A VICTORIAN LADY CYCLES THE WORLD

A VICTORIAN LADY CYCLES THE WORLD

Recollections of an Octogenarian

ISABEL G. HOMEWOOD

First edition entitled 'Recollections of an Octogenarian' published in 1932

This edition published 2018

Copyright © Dee Way and the family of Isabel Homewood 2018

The right of Dee Way and the descendants of Isabel Homewood to be identified as the author of this work has been asserted in accordance with the Copyright, Designs & Patents Act 1988.

All rights reserved. No part of this book may be reproduced, stored in a retrieval system, or transmitted in any form or by any means, electronic, electrostatic, magnetic tape, mechanical, photocopying, recording or otherwise, without the written permission of the copyright holder.

Published under licence by Brown Dog Books and

The Self-Publishing Partnership,
7 Green Park Station, Bath BA1 1JB

www.selfpublishingpartnership.co.uk

ISBN printed book: 978-1-78545-354-0

ISBN e-book: 978-1-78545-355-7

Cover design by Kevin Rylands

Internal design by Jenny Watson Design

The photo of Bowman's Lodge, Dartford (p18) is used with the kind permission of Dartford Library, Kent.

Printed and bound by CPI Group (UK) Ltd, Croydon, CR0 4YY

PREFACE

It is a great pleasure to see the release of this second edition of my great, great aunt's 'Recollections'. I had heard about this book for many years while growing up: a vivid record of one lady's life in Victorian and Edwardian times. I had been unable to find a copy to read until 2015, when my niece briefly lent me her copy and another niece shared a digital rendering of a library book.

The record of her early life and her tales of travels by bicycle are amazing, building on her unique relationship with Singer Bicycles who supplied her bespoke bicycles, due to her small stature. She was an enterprising lady, visiting New Zealand several times by steamer and sailing ship in the 19th Century and becoming a pioneering farmer in South Island as a newly wed. This first hand and engaging story of her life and travels, composed from her diaries, encapsulates her view of the various cultures she encountered as she cycled in many different parts of the world.

In keeping with the original version, the author's comments about the people she met and stayed with are unchanged, to reflect her view at the time. As such, its value as a unique record of the times is all the more interesting.

For clarity, her brother, referred to throughout as 'Pemberton' or 'Pem' was actually christened Walter Pemberton. He was my great grandfather who emigrated to New Zealand in 1863. My grandfather, of the same name, was the younger of her two nephews whom she mentions when cycling in Devon.

A few photographs and maps have been added to the original edition where they are relevant. I hope that this book will fascinate many others as much as it has myself, and inspire us all to travel: to see this world of different cultures and to meet with other free spirits. I am most grateful to Castle Publications, New Zealand and The Self-Publishing Partnership, Bath, UK for helping with the reprinting of this unusual personal history.

Dee Way

4 June 2018

CONTENTS

xi *Introduction by G. K. Chesterton*

1 CHAPTER I: Early years from 1844
Earliest memories – "Doddle" – Miss Mellon – Bowman's Lodge – Riding Astride – Dancing before the Prince Regent – At the Opera – The First Hunt – Dane Holes

19 CHAPTER II: Growing up
The Duke's funeral – The rocking-horse – Fräulein – The Lowther Arcade – The Lyttelton ghost – To darn Pem's socks – A cruel boy – The Crimean War – My mother's death – Mrs. Charles Dickens – Crinolines – Skating – Burglars – Pin-money – A cold ducking – My Stepmother – "Jim" – The Indian Mutiny – The Tooley Street fire – The Bickersteths – The Duke of Hamilton – "Psycho" – Whiteley's

59 CHAPTER III: Pioneer in New Zealand from 1867
Panama – In New Zealand – The new home – Dairy work – Good sport – Birds in the bush

– *"Homewood's swipes" – How work was done – The free life – Painting the house – "Betsy Douglas" – Quicksands – Swaggers and squatters – Many earthquakes – Back to England – Homeward bound – Pem – The Long Drive Mine – Gold seeking – Crossing the Wiapara – Maoris – A lovable people*

97   CHAPTER IV: Married life and archery
Music and archery – The Island of Herm – "Wanderlust" – The Prince of Wales

105   CHAPTER V: New Zealand again
New Zealand again – Shells and crabs – The bush

111   CHAPTER VI: Justice in Tasmania
My father's visit – Tasmania – Kangaroos – Guideless in the bush – At home again – Father's hat

123   CHAPTER VII: Tramp ship to Armenia, 1896
Lord Salisbury – Helping the Armenians – On board a tramp – At Bengazi – In Cairo – At the Pyramids – A plague of Arabs – The Sphinx – Landing at Jaffa – Alexandria – An Armenian home – Slaves and figs – Not a ratter – A rough passage – Divers commissions – Unsatisfactory Armenians

153   CHAPTER VIII: Cycling Europe, 1894
The happy cycle – Good distances – In France

– Arles – Mosquitoes – Frontier troubles –
The "Tramontana" – The road to Spezia –
The quarries at Carrara – Rain at Empoli.

173 CHAPTER IX: Midwifery training, 1897
Hospital training – A royal inspection –
A holiday duty.

181 CHAPTER X: Cycling through Italy
Between the ranks – Alaric – Calabria –
Unpleasantness in Sicily

187 CHAPTER XI: Corsica and Italy, 1898
Vendetta – Ajaccio – "A Lost Child"

193 CHAPTER XII: Madeira and Spain
Mrs. Grundy abroad – "Pomona" – Stones in Spain –
At a bull-fight

201 CHAPTER XIII: Visiting Scandinavia
Swedish miles – Stockholm – Norwegian courtesies

207 CHAPTER XIV: Cycling in Eastern Europe, 1904
Prussian Poland – Austrian Poland – The Vistula –
Polish peasants – Wild Jews – Picturesque Poland
– A night in Cracow – In Galicia – Carpathia –
A companion in Hungary – The Customs' chase

229 CHAPTER XV: Cycling round the world, 1910
In America – Niagara – New Zealand again – Maoris – Poor hospitality – A harsh journey – An insistent horseman – The fiords Among the lakes – Dead Man's Gully – A "swagger" – A night's lodging – An agricultural college

253 CHAPTER XVI: The Antipodes once more
The last visit – In the wilds

259 CONCLUSION: 1932: One woman's record

INTRODUCTION

I CONSIDER it a privilege to write this prefatory note; because I happen to regard the record of the lady who writes this book as much more remarkable, and even sensational, than any of those sensational newspaper stories of the feats of feminine pioneers, which will probably continue to be proclaimed in large letters in the popular press while there is a single thing that a woman has not yet done; and will display in larger and larger headlines the glory of the First Woman to Find the North Pole, or the First Woman to Climb Mount Everest. Without underrating for a moment the real personal qualities which must remain personal, even in so much advertised an adventure, it is not unfair to say that the new newspaper heroines have a thousand advantages which the heroine of this adventure not only never had but never expected and certainly never dreamed of demanding.

The modern heroines prepare for the process assisted by the very best technical advice, by the most elaborate modern machinery, in the full light of modern science, not to mention the light of modern publicity. The modern atmosphere is such that the beginning of the experiment is as conclusive as the conclusion; the send-off as triumphant as the triumph. Wealth in large quantities, and from very various sources, is available to support the enterprise at every stage. In short, the more recent lady adventurer has had the full benefit that comes from the best science and the worst journalism.

Mrs. Homewood set out on an ordinary bicycle to ride round the world, with no more fuss than if she had been riding round the parish pump. I do not imagine that she bothered very much about whether she was riding the very latest pattern of bicycle; or, if she did, it was in the same private and personal manner in which an ordinary housewife might wish to have the latest pattern of stove. She certainly had no backing from newspapers or newspaper millionaires; and the stages of her astonishing pilgrimage were certainly not recorded in headlines, and probably not recorded at all. Nay, it is only too probable that she actually preferred, such were the prejudices of her generation and breeding, not to be followed everywhere by a spotlight or announced at intervals by a megaphone. For she had, among her other eccentricities, an eccentricity that is rapidly fading from the world – something that was called the love of liberty, which is often akin to the love of loneliness. And it is becoming more and more obvious that liberty is every bit as much constrained by publicity, by cosmopolitan plans and commercial expectations, as by any restriction of any tyrannies or bigotries of the past. If it be Victorian to mind one's own business, and to regard one's own holiday as one's own business; if it be Victorian to prefer independence to indiscriminate and senseless eulogy from millions of total strangers who know nothing about the real story; if it be Victorian to wish to be free from mobs as well as monarchs, and from silly admiration as well as silly criticism, then certainly the Lady who wrote this story is a typical survival of the Victorian Age.

It is true that she set out on her adventures in a period when it was supposed (less universally than is commonly thought, and I fancy even less universally than she herself thinks), that a woman should remain at the fireside, and at an age when many such women were no longer expected to get out of the armchair. But I am not sure that she was not fortunate in the interlude of independence which she enjoyed after the worst of Puritan decorum was past and before the worst of plutocratic organisation had begun. Of such a personality, born in such a period, it is unnecessary to say that she has strong likes and dislikes of a personal kind; and strong opinions on many matters, with which it is not necessary that all her admirers should agree. The important fact remains that she was and is of a certain type; which the modern world is very fond of praising, but which it very seldom succeeds in perceiving when it is really there. The very words chosen to describe it confess to the confusion of modern thought. It is customary to talk of such persons as pioneers; mainly because of a particular metaphor of Walt Whitman, who had at least the excuse of living in a country where pioneering had often meant the exploration of virgin forests and untrodden wastes. But the metaphor is false; a pioneer is not a man who leads an army, he is merely a man who clears away obstacles on the particular path which the commander has already chosen. It is unfortunate that the alternative term adventurer, and still more the term adventuress, has been twisted into a false and degraded sense. Indeed, that perversion of that word is perhaps the worst witness that remains against the real vices of the Victorian era. But if anyone wants to know how very adventurous could be the virtues of the Victorian era, and who were the real forerunners of what we call the modern freedom, he could not do better than read this book; especially as, whatever happens to the movement that follows, the forerunners at least were free.

G. K. CHESTERTON

CHAPTER I
EARLY YEARS FROM 1844

I AM eighty-eight years of age, and in my long life I have seen so many people and such great changes in the way of travelling and mode of dress, etc., that I think a short account of my experiences will probably interest many of my friends and perhaps some people I do not even know.

Old people have a livelier remembrance of their extreme youth than of any other period of their lives. Why, I cannot tell! As far as I am concerned, I do not feel old.

Most people when I was young led very drab and uneventful lives; there were not many red-letter days or events to make note of. Any change from the tedious monotony was looked forward to, especially by the young folk, for a long time in advance. A journey was not a thing to plan on the spur of the moment; every detail was mapped out weeks beforehand. Invitations were issued for a party several weeks previously.

Children were kept very strictly in the nursery and bullied by the nurses. The preparation for an after-dinner visit to the drawing-room was far from pleasant. I remember well how we had our hands and faces washed regardless how much soap went into our eyes. Our hair was brushed and combed, a good pull being given to any knots, and then we were ruthlessly pushed into clean frocks, quite regardless whether we wanted to go to the drawing-room or not. On Sundays we were allowed to go down to dessert. I can remember details of my youth; I can also remember details of my later life quite distinctly, so it is very evident that I am not senile yet!

I was sixty-six years of age when I started my tour round the world on my bicycle. The doctor, when he came on board at Boston to examine the passengers before they were allowed to land, was obliged to class me with the "senile," as I was over sixty! As you may well imagine, I was highly indignant. The doctor was very charming and did his best to soothe my wounded feelings. I suppose he, poor man, was merely carrying out regulations.

If my readers do not feel interested in the details of how children and young people were treated in my childhood, they may just skip a few of the next pages.

There were not often breaks in the monotony of our lives as children. My father's habits were very irregular, so parties and such-like fun could not be indulged in, as nothing could be fixed up weeks beforehand, as was the fashion. Even breakfast and dinner could not be relied upon at a definite time. We had few or no toys to relieve the monotony of our existence. The great number of toys, and expensive ones, that the present generation of children are given is one of the most striking differences between their lives and ours; but I doubt if they are any happier.

I was born in January 1844, and my recollections go back to 1847. We lived then in Lonsdale Square, London. We were then a family of four children. Ellen was the eldest; then came two boys, William and Pemberton; I was the youngest. Later, a brother called Henry died when quite a baby, and two sisters, whom I can scarcely remember, Emily and Alice, when aged eight and fifteen. When I was eight years of age another little sister, Edith, arrived. She is still living.

I can well remember my younger brother knocking my head through the nursery window! Another vivid recollection is the sound of gulping from the corner of the room, and a frightened exclamation, "I have swallowed my farthing!" from the same brother. The nurses were evidently very concerned, for they rushed and fetched my mother. I was very proud to be able to tell the time before the brother of the farthing fame.

I sat on the hearthrug like many a child before and since, and poured over Mavor's spelling book to learn my task of words of two syllables.

Nurse's threats instilled most terrible childish fears. I was told that if I was naughty I would be given to the butcher, and I imagined myself cut up into joints and carried in a tray such as the butcher boys carried the meat in from house to house; and seeing them often from the nursery window did not help to calm my fears.

Once, when out for a walk with the nursery governess, I got lost in a crowd that was watching a Punch and Judy show, and I well remember yelling, "Take care of me, take care of me," which some kindly soul did, and soon succeeded in finding the governess, who was nearly as alarmed as I was.

Our chief friends in the Square were the Grays. Mr. Gray was a barrister, as was my father. The Grays remained close friends for many years. Mr. Gray had a squint, and I never could tell when he was addressing me. After we left Lonsdale Square, the Grays moved to Gloucester Crescent, Regent's Park, to a house opposite the one then occupied by Mrs. Charles Dickens.

Mr. Gray became solicitor to the Treasury, and I suppose had a good stipend. He was left a widower with ten children, and was able to allow his grown-up daughters £100 a year for pin-money.

My father kept ponies and a four-wheel carriage. It had a small seat which let up and down. This was where I sat when driving with my parents, and the three elder children sat upon the back seat. I was rather afraid of those ponies; they used to "play up" in the Square when being brought to the house. But I loved being put upon their backs. "Doodle" was a pony straight from the Shetland Islands. He was in shape more like a hunter than a Shetland pony – he could not have been much bigger than a Mastiff. A special small gig was made for

"Doodle" and it had a tiny seat in it for me, like that in the four-wheel carriage.

My maternal grandmother often stayed with us when we were at Lonsdale Square, and I still have a vivid recollection of one of her visits. We children often went to see her in her bedroom. One day the three eldest clamoured for certain china ornaments which were on her mantelpiece, and she gave them. All the time I was dreadfully afraid one of the elders would fix on the ornament I wanted, but fortunately they did not do so and I was either too shy or remembered I had been taught not to ask for things. My grandmother was also my godmother, and I thought surely she will ask me to choose one of her ornaments; but she did not do so, and I went away feeling very, very hurt. Oddly enough, I have that very ornament I coveted amongst my treasures now. It must have been quite by chance that it was sent to me a few years ago, when a division of china took place, occasioned by deaths. With that said piece of china came the piece Ellen had chosen, which I had always intended to offer to her, but she died before I had an opportunity to carry out my intention.

The last memory of Lonsdale Square was of driving away to a house in the county of Kent, about fifteen miles from London. I know we stopped at Bedford Row, I expect to pick up my father; his chambers were there at that time. Soon afterwards he moved to Chancery Lane, to be nearer the Chancery Courts.

Our move to the country took place in September 1847, when I was three years and nine months old. Our new house was called "Bowman's Lodge". When we first went to live there, there were no trains or other public conveyances. My father was obliged to drive up to town, returning every other day. The house was a funny old rambling place built mostly of wood. I think there must have been a brick cottage on the site, and the wooden additions were run up for the accommodation of the Prince Regent (afterwards George IV), who held his toxophilite[1] meetings there, hence the name of the house.

Miss Mellon, the actress, made her debut at Bowman's Lodge at the time the Prince Regent rented the house. Her portrait was at one time at the Lodge, and it was sold at Dorchester (*vide* Roach Smith's *Retrospections*). Miss Mellon married Mr. Coutts, the banker, and was left a very rich widow. Later she married the Duke of St. Albans. My father was distantly related to the Duke of St. Albans through the Cracroft family. There were many skits upon her marriage. One in particular was, "A fat woman with breasts like a melon with a slice cut in it." No doubt the caricature is still in existence. My father remembered seeing it in a shop in Cheapside. After she became Duchess of St. Albans, my grandfather and mother used to visit at the Duke's mansion in London, and my grandfather used to go to Newbury Park, the Duke's country seat. The Duke was the hereditary Grand Falconer of England.

---

1. Archery

The author's father, William Cracroft Fooks, Q.C. (driving) and servants outside Bowmans Lodge, Dartford Heath, about 1870.

When I was a young girl, my Uncle Henry, then living at Holloway, used to take me for his Sunday walk to show me the tomb of the Duke. As far as I can remember, it was of red granite. My uncle would then explain our relationship through the Duke's first wife.

The Prince Regent rented Bowman's Lodge from Lady Salteson (I think that was her name, but I am not quite sure), who sold it to my maternal grandfather, Mr. Walker, then a solicitor in the town of Dartford, and it became the summer residence of my grandfather and his family. It was a queer old rambling place. There were a few lofty rooms and several smaller ones; these smaller rooms served as nurseries and afterwards as the girls' bedrooms. The whole building was rather like a rabbit warren. The part of the house that fascinated us children most was the semi-basement and underground passages, the latter being filled with all sorts of lumber, dear to a child's heart. There were numerous nooks and corners, real bogie holes, all lending themselves to lovely sport, such as "hide and seek," "hare and hounds," "touch last," etc. In fact, a very happy hunting ground on wet days, and on wet Sundays my father used to join us.

Sometimes in very wet weather the underground passages were flooded and bricks had to be laid down as stepping-stones. Of course, that greatly enhanced the fun, for us at least! We were quite regardless of the mud and mess we carried all over the house. The servants always seemed to enter into the fun when the "hare" with "hounds" in full cry took refuge in the kitchen or nursery premises, so they knew if they grumbled at the mess they would lose a good deal of fun in the future.

Bowman's Lodge was in a very neglected state when we arrived there, and we were obliged to lead a sort of picnic existence just at first. I do not remember any maid-servants being there after our fifteen-mile drive, so all the help my mother got was from a groom and his wife who had been with my father since his marriage.

The first night we four children slept in one large room. Early the next morning we managed to dress ourselves and went out to explore the grounds, which seemed to have been ploughed or dug up preparatory to making a garden. Ellen led the way, followed by Willie and Pem; my small self came last, trying to take big strides and keep in their footsteps, as Ellen said a scolding was in store for us if we trod on the damp ground. At the end of the ploughed ground there were some railings fencing off a nice paddock. We soon managed to wriggle through the rails. In the paddock were beautiful clumps of trees, between which the Prince Regent, no doubt, had his targets pitched, just as we had ours later on. This is all that I can remember of the first day in our new home.

Nurses were soon installed, but we had our meals with our mother. The family doctor called one day while we were having breakfast and to our disgust prohibited us having sugar in our cocoa, but he rose in our estimation when he told mother to "let us live like little pigs." I suppose we must have been delicate. I for one followed the doctor's prescription to the letter! I found my way to the cowshed and milked all the milk I wanted for myself, little guessing how useful the "art" would prove to me in years to come in New Zealand.

Just beyond the garden was a large fruit plantation. It was sub-let when we first arrived, so of course we were forbidden to go into it. The temptation was too strong for us to obey. There was only an old man in charge, and he had a wheezy cough which we could hear from afar; he also had something red about his attire, which showed up well through the gooseberry bushes, so we got good warning of his approach and fled! I rather think the tenant of that orchard must have been in arrears with his rent, for we were never punished for committing these daily raids.

My parents paid a short visit to Paris, and left us in charge of an aunt who had just returned from India. This aunt was not fond of children, and childlike, I soon discovered her aversion. I have no kindly recollections of her. Once she banished me to the nursery because I could not swallow some tough beef she had provided for our dinner. Years were slowly crawling by. Another brother was born, and nurseries were installed again; but he died when he was only a few months' old.

Ellen at this time considered me old enough to hire me as nurse to her wax doll. I was supposed to dress and undress that doll daily, but soon had the misfortune to break its arm. I made matters worse by trying to sew the arm on again. I raided the nursery work-box for needle and cotton, but the kid on the arm was very rotten and I had to confess to what had happened, and was then and there dismissed without my wages. I never really cared for dolls, and converted my doll's house into stables. I monopolised a large hollow oak tree which stood in the garden, and in the hollow I kept sticks, which I made believe were horses. An old broomstick that had a hole at one end, through which I passed a string to serve as a bridle, was a great treasure. My mother caught me riding it astride and severely reprimanded me; it was such an unusual thing for my mother to do that I felt very guilty. How ideas have changed since then!

Our head nurse was a great bully, and Ellen aided her

in trying to bully me. Our nursery was long and narrow, and much of the furniture was against the wall, so I was well able to run along from chair to chair or table or chest, and kick out at them as I went! I was considered to be very naughty, and my father told me that if that particular nurse (the bully) left on account of my bad behaviour, he would never forgive me. To me that was a dreadful threat.

I think my mother must have got an inkling that all was not as it should be in the nursery, for one day she paid an unexpected visit and found Emily in a corner in disgrace. My mother wished to know what she was being punished for, and found she had called the nurse "a bull." My mother released the child, and the nurse left in consequence. My father never even scolded Emily, but had I been the culprit I was never to be forgiven! – a bit of injustice that rankled in my youthful bosom and caused me to be a bit jealous of my little sister in future. Ellen never seemed to forgive me for the accident that befell her doll's arm; in fact, we were always quarrelling. I remember my father sitting me up in a high chair and asking me what my grievances were. I answered in a childish way, "Ellen is so very disagreeable."

When I was about six, I was taken out of the nursery and allowed to run about the house and grounds. It was a lovely life, except that I had no companions, and I was not allowed to play with the gardener's children.

At that time my mother was teaching Ellen and me. The boys were at a boarding school. When out driving we often passed the village school, and I watched with envious eyes the children trouping out from school and looking so bright and so happy. How I longed to be at that school! Although the head mistress was named Miss Scrag, that did not deter me from wishing to be one of her pupils. My mother used to threaten to send me there as a punishment, but I never succeeded, although I tried very hard to be naughty enough for the threat to be carried out.

During my solitary wanderings, I often found my way to the kitchen. There was an old woman who came to give occasional help when there was extra work to do, and I liked listening to the yarns she told. One story was about how she used to dance on a stage that had been in front of the drawing-room windows at Bowman's Lodge when the Prince Regent was there. Her parents forbade her to do it any more, but she said a carriage was sent to fetch her after her parents had gone to bed, and that she was taken to Bowman's Lodge to dance, and taken home again before her parents were up in the morning!

At the bottom of what we called the long walk there was an old pollard oak, which I used to climb and in which I often hid. From that oak I could watch the gipsies arrive and encamp, but too far from my hiding-place to hear their conversation. I saw them collect wood and light their fires – I think that it was watching them that imbued me with the wish to travel and see all I could of the world. During my rambles in the garden, I learned a great deal about the birds and their nests; I even managed to catch them on their nests, and took them to my mother and begged her to let me keep them in a cage, but she wisely ordered me to take them back to the nests. Once I took a blackbird and, at another time, a redstart off their nests and carried them to my mother, and, strangely enough, when I released them they did not forsake their nests. The servants told me I could catch birds easily if I put salt on their tails, but I found I could do better without it. I thought it was owing to the salt having melted in my hand that I was unable to put it on the birds' tails!

My mother gave me a canary, which I was to feed and care for, but I am ashamed to say I neglected it, and one morning I found it dead with no food and a dirty cage and green water. I gave the poor bird a very grand funeral, and really did feel sorry for my neglect.

I was very devoted to my mother and tried to show my love by taking her the first-fruits of the orchard. I pinched the early plums till they were soft, so hoping to see my mother enjoy them. It was a great sacrifice on my part for my mother did not seem to like them very much and I would willingly have gobbled them all up.

I do not think my mother was very strong – she was often ailing. She had a beautiful voice that had been well trained. I loved to hear her sing, but I could not often persuade her to do so. My favourite song was the Schubert's "Erlking." She often went to the Italian Opera, where she and my father had a box which held four. The four generally consisted of my father and mother, Ellen and a girl friend of hers. On one occasion, when I was seven, my sister's friend was away, and I was taken in her place. Our dresses were made of white tucked book muslin with black ruching round the neck and sleeves and broad black silk sashes, for we were in mourning for my father's mother. We drove all the way to London in our own carriage, dressed, and had an oyster supper at my father's chambers, then at 30 Chancery Lane before going to the opera. His chambers were on the fourth floor; the stairs were very narrow, with banisters, which I confounded with my father being a barrister. I had seen his wig and gown, and thought that his occupation was sliding up and down the banisters in his wig and gown. This quaint idea remained firmly fixed in my mind for some time, as we were not allowed to ask questions.

At the opera Sontag and Lablache sang. The latter was a very fat man. The singing and the ballet enthralled me while I was awake, but I am ashamed to say I slept a greater part of the time.

How my father found the carriage in the crush outside the Opera House was very bewildering to me; I thought it wonderfully clever of him. I suffered dreadfully from thirst during the drive home, and begged to be allowed to get out of the carriage and drink from a wayside duck-pond which was covered over with green slime, but I had to wait till I got home. No thought was given to my misery. It would have been so easy to stop at an inn and get me a glass of water. I think more consideration would have been shown to the modern child in a like plight.

My father always thought it was good training for children that they should learn to endure. He never seemed in the least concerned if we were thrown from our ponies. He said we must learn how to fall. At that time I was riding "Doddle". He was a perfect little devil – reared and kicked directly he got outside the gate on to the open heath. Sometimes he took it into his head to scamper back when only halfway across the heath. My mother, who anticipated trouble or an accident, often waited at the gate and let "Doddle" and me in. When my father returned he was very angry. Sometimes he would allow the groom to lead "Doddle" with my small self mounted until we got to a narrow lane, when I used to manage without the groom. My riding dress then was a green habit with a lot of buttons, a beaver hat, and my brother's outgrown duck trousers for underneath wear.

My first hunt was on a very large, quiet white pony, and I was laughed at and called a fly on an elephant, which upset my dignity very considerably. I went to my second hunt on "Doddle." I had three falls jumping, and a fourth while riding home after the hunt, owing to sheer fatigue. I fell in a ploughed field and let my pony go, which was considered a fearful crime, as we were always told to hang on to the bridle when thrown. My father and Ellen scampered after and caught "Doddle", while I sat under a hedge and cried. Our doctor's son came along and laughed at me. I was made to remount and ride home, which was about another three miles.

My father must have taken to riding to hounds soon after we came to Bowman's Lodge on Dartford Heath. I was eight years of age when my parents gave a hunt breakfast. The harriers were hunted by Messrs. Robert and John Russell, and the kennels were at the residence of their mother at Horton Kirby.

The Hunt breakfast must have been rather a large affair, as non-hunting friends were asked to the meet. As this meet was the first in the neighbourhood, the ground was quite unknown to the Masters and Huntsmen. There were numerous holes, now called Dane Holes, in the open fields and woods and in the thick hedges, all unprotected. The "natives" knew their whereabouts so it had not been considered necessary to fence them round. As soon as breakfast was over and the Stirrup Cup handed round, a start was made across the heath and fields towards Bexley.

My two brothers and I were mounted. The boys soon went off on their own and I was left with my father, who always kept at a distance from the hounds and members of the Hunt. He persisted in riding so close to the Dane Holes that I was in mortal terror all the time. My fears were increased by one of the Masters telling my father that one of his boys was down a hole, but fortunately just then I spied my two brothers in the distance.

The boy mistaken for one of my brothers was named Mathews. His mother and sisters had been at the breakfast. Someone rode off immediately to inform them the boy was killed, upon which they went back to their home at Bexley Heath. No sooner had they reached home than the boy appeared! The truth was, the boy in trying to follow the hounds made for a gap in a very thick hedge and tried to get through, but his pony stuck, so he dismounted to lead it through, when suddenly the pony vanished and he found himself caught on the branch of a tree that grew straight across the hidden mouth of a Dane Hole. The pony's back was broken, and it had to be shot.

Some of the Dane Holes had, for children, terrifying names. One in Darnwood, not far from Swanscombe, was called "Clapper Napper's Hole". My father often rode there and would go close to the edge and, as I had not complete control over Doddle, I was obliged to follow in his wake, which frightened me very much. There was another hole in Shepherd's Lane, leading from Dartford Heath to Dartford that was called "Sound Hole." Whenever going past it on foot, we threw stones down it to listen to them hitting the sides; and, judging from the time the stones took to reach the bottom, the hole must have been pretty deep. Rumour had it that this hole was the receptacle of the bad meat from the Dartford butchers, and other refuse, besides our stones.

In those days nobody seemed interested in, or appeared to want to know, the origin of these holes. Not till twenty years later did one hear of speculation regarding them, when some personal friends of mine set to work to explore them. Some in Jordan's Wood had quite narrow entrances, and they were able to descend by steps cut in the sides. Some they found were connected with caves. Later on, the caves at Chislehurst were found and explored; they are said to run right under Blackheath, and are thought to be connected with the Dane Holes in other parts of Kent. I don't know what conclusions archaeologists have come to about these holes, but they seem to me to be natural formations and not the work of prehistoric man, as was at one time thought.

There was in those days, when we hunted with the harriers, a paper mill with a mill pond in the neighbourhood; and I can remember seeing a hare with hounds in full cry jump into the mill pond and swim across it, but when the hare landed on the farther side the poor bedraggled creature was soon despatched by the mob of excited mill hands who had collected on hearing the hounds.

Bowmans Lodge, Dartford, in its heyday.

CHAPTER II

GROWING UP

My eighth year was rather a momentous one. My parents gave their first ball – It was a very grand affair, and all arrangements were made on a very lavish scale. Rout-seats[2] covered with Turkey twill were erected round the room to allow space for the dancing. An orchestra was built, also covered with red twill, and a military band was engaged from Woolwich. The floor was covered with a dancing cloth. I think the ball was given in honour of my father's youngest sister, who was staying with us before going to Valparaiso, where she eventually married and lived for many years. Ellen's dress was made of red tarlatan, and the dressmaker who came to the house to work managed to screw a dress for me out of the material.

There was only accommodation in the house for the young ladies who came from London or a distance, so the

---

2. Removable seats used for temporary seating.

young men who were unable to return home that night were offered a shake-down in the laundry, where my father had beds put round the ironing-room. Many of my father's clients, among others, came from town and availed themselves of that rather original accommodation. I had a lovely time; I danced every dance. One of my partners was a Mr. Henniker, a very big man, the tallest man in the room – quite 6ft. 4in. After our dance he carried me on his shoulder.

That dance was such a success that it gave an idea for the formation of a dance club, the members of which met at each other's houses in turn for dancing every Wednesday evening. I was always taken to these dances. Some of the young ladies took music with them, and of course had to be asked to sing or play. Amateur music was then, as often is the case now, very bad. How grateful we ought to be for the gramophone these days.

The Prince-Consort was highly musical, and the quality of amateur performers greatly improved during his time.

I was taken to the Exhibition of 1851, when I was seven years old. I remember seeing the Kohinoor diamond, then in its original uncut state; also a bedstead which could be set to time, like an alarm clock, to tip its occupants out, appealed greatly to me. In March 1931 the Committee of the Persian Art Exhibition gave an "At Home" and tea to people who had been to the Exhibition of 1851. As I had been to the Exhibition of 1851, I attended this "At Home". Many of those present had been taken as babies in arms and had no recollection whatever of the Exhibition. One old man of ninety-five with whom I had a chat was only able to remember a big mirror at the entrance to the Exhibition. I got into conversation with another guest, and we wandered far away from the Exhibition of 1851; but for all that she was most interesting to talk to. She told me that her great-uncle had been steward on Sir John Franklin's ship in the Arctic Expedition. And I was able to tell her that I could distinctly remember that my mother used to ask my father when he returned from town if he had called on his aunt, Lady Franklin, to enquire news of her husband's search expedition. Lady Franklin had been a Miss Cracroft, sister to my father's mother. My father always expressed himself indebted to Sir John Franklin for being allowed the use of his library at the time he was a clerk in the service of the East India Company before he decided to take up Law as a profession.

The Duke of Wellington died the following year, and my father took my two brothers to see the funeral procession pass St. Paul's Cathedral.

As I said before, my brothers were sent to a boarding school when they were very young. They were only eight and ten years of age. At first they went to Thame Grammar School, in Oxfordshire. My uncle, father's eldest brother, was then head master. He was educated at Winchester, and from there entered New College, Oxford, where he was made a fellow of his college. He married, so consequently lost the benefit derived from his fellowship, and was given a curacy in a village in Kent. Later he became head master of the Thame Grammar School, then belonging to New College. There, he and his family lived for years in the beautiful old house. The original grammar school was converted into a girls' school when a new grammar school was built. I shall later have much to write about that uncle and his family, as many a happy time was spent with them when I was old enough to pay visits.

The first visit I ever paid was evidently not considered by the "grown-ups" a great success! I was only about five when a younger brother of my father's and his young wife, who often came to Bowman's Lodge, took me back with them to Holloway where they lived with the wife's parents. Having no children of their own, they made a great pet of me, an almost new experience which I much appreciated and took advantage of on every possible occasion. I declined to go to bed at night, and had to be carried, kicking and screaming with all my might.

I was given a penny a day to spend at a toy-shop nearby. The only thing I wanted was a rocking-horse, and I yelled and screamed to become the possessor of one. The servant who took me every morning to the shop left me there, evidently ashamed to have anything to do with such a naughty child. Directly I was alone, I dried my tears and pleaded with the woman in the shop for a rocking-horse, and thought her very hard hearted not to give it to me, for I knew if I worried my mother long enough I always got what I wanted. The servant was sent to bring me back to my uncle's house, and as soon as I realised I was to go without the rocking-horse, I started kicking and screaming again.

Although I was very happy with my uncle and aunt and enjoyed the spoiling, I felt very homesick. One day, with great joy, I spied my father hiding behind the door when I was sent for to go to the drawing room. He had come to take me home. Of course, no sooner was I at home than I wanted to return to the petting and spoiling. At home I was one of many and there was a nursery. My uncle and aunt soon had their own children, and it was very many years before I paid them another visit.

In my mother's wardrobe, when I was between the age of seven and eight, I spied a riding-whip, and thought it must be intended for Ellen or an aunt who was staying with us at the time.

To my great delight I discovered that it was meant for me, but to gain it I was to keep a diary for a whole week. That diary lies before me now, and attached to it my father's comments. In the diary, the only variations from lessons morning and evening was "Quarrelled with Ellen". Whether that caused my father to write in the diary that I had not earned the whip and must try again, I do not know, but a future diary, which unfortunately I have not kept, earned me the whip. This same whip I gave a few years ago to a grand-niece who was learning to ride, and I am now sending her the first diary, which I found lately when looking through some old letters and papers.

Ellen and I had been taught by my mother. Music lessons we had twice a week from a master who came from Woolwich. Dancing and callisthenics we learned at a school a few miles distant.

Suddenly a great change took place in my life. It was the arrival of a German governess. She could not speak English, and she and my mother conversed in French. She was engaged not to speak English to us, but make us speak German. I think the German governess must have been engaged because I had been very naughty and given my mother a great deal of trouble. This made me very sad, and I made up my mind to try to be good.

Fraulein was very badly marked with smallpox, which she had suffered from as a child. Our first meeting was not quite a happy one. She tried to kiss me and I always disliked being kissed, and more so by her on account of the pock-marks. The following day we got on better. She was up early, and we met in the garden, as I was always an early riser too. She taught me several German words that morning.

From the time I was big enough to hold the tea-pot, I was up early to see that my father had his breakfast. It was the privilege of the eldest daughter to do this, but my sister was of a more indolent disposition, and it irked her to be up when breakfast had been ordered for 7.30 – a frequent occurrence, especially in winter – and my parents had established the rule that whichever of us was at their door first should have the keys and make the tea. Ellen tried very hard to be up, and never could guess what awakened me in an adjoining room. Of course, I never told her, but it was the noise of opening a drawer to get a hairbrush that woke me up. I immediately jumped out of bed and scrambled into my clothes, and by the time Ellen opened her door I was ready for a race through night and day nurseries to my mother's door, quite regardless that my dress, that hooked behind, was gaping open. I invariably got there first and was given the keys, so was able to make and pour out the tea. By the time Fraulein arrived, Ellen had ceased even trying to be first.

Fraulein appreciated those early morning walks in the garden; the birds were singing and everything looked very beautiful. It was a very good start for the lessons that followed later in the day. Ellen did not frequent the schoolroom regularly. She was already old enough to visit a great deal, and when at home in the winter she was hunting with father.

Whether my mother liked walking or unselfishly left the ponies for my father's use, I do not know; I only remember her driving when she went to the station to meet my father, the railway by that time having reached Woolwich. Shortly afterwards a station was built at Erith, and later at Dartford. I remember many a walk with my mother to a shop in Dartford, two miles distant. Ellen must have been away from home, so she took me as her companion. One such excursion was to buy a birthday present for Ellen. It was to be a scent bottle containing salts (young ladies were given to fainting in those days). The jeweller my mother went to had none in stock that she liked, so he produced a second-hand one that she immediately recognised as her own. It had been stolen and sold to the jeweller, who of course returned it to my mother.

That same day I saw a Japanese doll in a small shop, and took a fancy to it – at the time I only possessed a mutilated wooden one. The first thing that the boys would do when they came home for their holidays was to make for my dolls; if of wax, the eyes were poked out; if of wood, the eyes were cut out, and they were otherwise disfigured. My mother bought me the Japanese doll, which as soon as the holidays commenced met with the usual fate. We must have been doing considerable trade with Japan, even in those days, for a small country town shop to have Japanese goods. Once, after a visit to our dentist, my mother took me to the Lowther Arcade in the Strand, long since demolished, and allowed me to choose anything I liked. My choice was a little ink-bottle, and she bought me a big wax doll besides; but I never cared for it.

Among my mother's acquaintances was a family of the name of Applegath. Mr. Applegath was the inventor of the first *Times* printing press, which I believe is still in the museum of old machines at South Kensington. Mr. Applegath was well paid for his invention, but at the time I am speaking of he and his family of three daughters were living on a pension that *The Times* office was allowing him out of gratitude and in recognition of the benefit they had derived from his invention.

His daughters were always rather bitter towards their father. Their mother had died very young, and all her money had been wasted in patenting other inventions that had proved unsuccessful. When he was a very old man he often came to see my father with some new invention he was anxious to patent. But as he had great faith in my father's opinion, he (my father) was generally able to dissuade him from spending more money, for these inventions of his later life were quite useless.

My father was well known for his knowledge of patent law. I remember him telling us, when the Aerated Bread Company was first floated, that bread was going to be made by machinery. The A.B.C. was one of the earliest companies registered under the Act of 1862, which codified the law relating to Joint Stock Companies. He also had patent business to do with the first sewing machine made in England (Thomas's), and was presented with a model machine. This reminds me that at Colon I saw a "Howe" the first sewing machine invented by an American.

Mr. Applegath had been a very rich man; it was only his useless inventions that had brought him to poverty. At his own expense he had built the Roman Catholic Chapel at Crayford. His wife was a Protestant, and expressed the wish when she was dying that her children should be brought up in the Protestant faith. The Applegaths lived in a house said to be haunted by the ghost of Lord Lyttelton.

The story runs that Lord Lyttelton, who was at that time stationed in India, was very intimate with the then owner of the house, whose name I forget. Lord Lyttelton was in the habit of turning up at this friend's house at unexpected moments without ceremony. One day his friend saw him approaching the house and ordered his room to be prepared for him, but to his astonishment when he looked again he had vanished. It transpired later that Lord Lyttelton had died in India the very moment his friend thought he saw him in Dartford. I slept in the room he was supposed to haunt, out of bravado, but nothing happened to disturb my slumbers but my own fears. The house had a nice old-fashioned garden; also a good piece of water, where I learned to row and fish, and also used to skate later.

Near where the Applegaths lived were the powder mills owned by Messrs. Piggou & Wilks, who lived on the premises. Explosions often occurred, and as a child I was dreadfully frightened that one might happen while we were there. To walk there, my mother used to go by a lane which was called the Manor Way. The first time I went with her she told me the name of the lane, and I asked her if people came there to learn manners. She only laughed. Mrs. Wilks was at home when we called, and showed us a Christmas tree she was "dressing," then called a German tree. They had been introduced into England by the Prince Consort, and were quite a novelty at the time. Mrs. Wilks showed us all the presents, and I decided in my own mind what I would like to have; but unfortunately I did not get that particular gift when the party came off. Mrs. Wilks had no children. She was always very kind to me and invited me to all her parties.

Later on, when the Wednesday dances my mother helped to initiate were given up at her death, Mrs. Wilks had gatherings every Wednesday, a dinner party first and a dance afterwards, to which I always went, although I was only twelve years of age. My father married again about fifteen months after my mother's death. My stepmother tried to put a stop to my going to Mrs. Wilks's gatherings – she probably thought we could be more profitably occupied at home! We girls had never done any plain needlework, just fancy work, knitting, and crocheting taught by Fraulein.

Almost the first Wednesday after my father's second marriage, he forbade me to go to Mrs. Wilks's party – he said I was to stay at home and darn Pem's socks. The following Wednesday I was allowed to go and Mrs. Wilks, before the whole room of guests, asked me why I had not been on the previous Wednesday. And I told her in a very audible voice, "I was kept at home to darn Pem's socks". A suppressed titter went round the room, and from that time my father did not keep me away from those gatherings.

Father used to be blamed by his friends for taking his daughters out hunting, as it was not considered "the thing" for girls to hunt. Father, dressed for hunting, would sometimes pass through the schoolroom where Fraulein was trying to teach me. I was her only pupil then, as the younger ones were still in the nursery. I used to jump from my chair and cling to him, begging and praying to go out hunting with him. I often followed him to the stable yard before he would give in, and then I only got my own way by the groom saying "Billy" wanted exercise. That settled the matter. I flew to get into my habit. Naturally, Fraulein was furious.

When morning lessons were over, Fraulein took us for a walk, usually to the post office, as she was anxious to see if there were any letters for her from Germany.

There was no postal delivery in the country in those days. As this walk took place just before dinner, I was always very hungry, and most of my pocket money went on gingerbreads sold at the baker's shop next to the post office. Gingerbreads were at that time 10d. per pound, and I used to buy a quarter of a pound and share them with Fraulein. My pocket money was 4d. a week, out of which I was supposed to buy my gloves, which of course I never did. That allowance was at times supplemented by silver coins being placed on the mantelpiece. These coins varied from 2s. 6d. to a threepenny piece, to be claimed or not on a Saturday evening, according to the report Fräulein gave as to my progress.

Morning lessons always began by my having to repeat the lessons I had learned overnight. The books from which I had learned were in a pile in front of Fraulein: a little German poetry, a piece of a French verb, a German declension, some geography and history, etc. Every piece I did not know or had forgotten was marked, and I had to write it out six times for an imposition after lessons were over in the evening. As I hated learning by heart, I soon gave up the attempt. I much preferred to scribble out all my lessons six times. Fräulein sat in the schoolroom with me while I wrote, and I gloated over the knowledge that she would much have preferred to sit with the others. When Saturdays came round, I did not often get a coin off the mantelpiece.

On the opposite side of the heath to Bowman's Lodge, in a picturesque cottage, a family named Hayward lived.

There were three children of about the ages of my elder sister and two brothers, and they were their great friends. Shortly after the arrival of Fräulein, Mr. Hayward got into financial difficulties, and my mother invited Mrs. Hayward and the three children to stay with us. The eldest boy, a little older than Willie, was the ringleader of the pranks they played on me. He was really a very cruel boy and led me a dreadful life. He used to get up early in the morning just to mustard the nose of my pet kitten or to water my cactus. But still worse, he would put a cushion over my head and keep it there till I was nearly stifled. Once he got some rancid fat from the kitchen and rubbed it on my arms, the smell of which made me sick. For this he was reprimanded by my mother.

Another of his jokes was to get the other boys to join him in hunting me. They armed themselves with lilac switches, and when I was out walking quite demurely with Fräulein, they would spring out from the shrubs and with their switches aim for my legs. To the horror of the governess, I would fly for my life and generally managed to take refuge with my mother. On one occasion I was thwarted by closed doors and could not get to her, but I just managed to slip into the closet and bolt the door. This closet was in one of the funny underground passages of the old house. The door had a glass window so I made long noses at the boys and shouted cheeky remarks, although I knew from their suppressed laughter that they were all ready and waiting to pounce out upon me with their lilac switches. Lesson time came, and I knew I would be in disgrace if I did not go to the schoolroom so I called out that they would be a set of cowards if they hit me, and walked out looking far braver than I felt, and they were so flabbergasted that they let me pass unmolested.

My tormentor went into the army and rose to be a General. He died recently, over ninety years of age. We made friends in after years, but when I was a child I really hated him, he was so very cruel. I often wondered what sort of a husband and father he made!

The arrival of a younger brother of my father from India caused a diversion from the storms that had arisen in the schoolroom. He brought all sorts of good things from India, at that time hardly known of at home, such as guava jelly, pickled mangoes, and curry powder. To my great delight, he spent much of his time in the schoolroom melting lead over the fire and casting bullets. He told us that he was going to the Crimea to fight. The Crimean War had just commenced. For some reason or other he was not drafted out there, neither did he see service during the Indian Mutiny, but he went out later and helped to clear matters up there. He was married before he returned to India. My parents and Ellen went to the wedding in Brighton, and stayed there for a while afterwards. To my great delight they sent for me. I well remember the old chain pier and the souvenirs made out of shells. The sea did not impress me.

The Crimean War cast a gloom over the whole neighbourhood. Most of the young men we knew went out, and in many cases did not live to return.

My father's two hunters were commandeered, but he was soon able to buy four more horses straight from a boat from Germany. One was intended for a brougham horse for my Mother, and the other three to combine farm work and hunting. My father had just then rented a small farm. He always spent his vacation at home and amused himself with farming. The first time he did any ploughing he used two ponies, one of which I rode and guided, and I am perfectly sure I guided quite straight; but father's furrow was very shallow and zigzaggy. I can still see his puzzled expression. A harrow rake he managed to manipulate better. I spent those farming days with him, as Fräulein was having her long holiday at the time. I must have been very small when I helped with the harrow rake, as I had to jump up to the handle to catch it when the rake required clearing of the weeds.

My father put me in charge of the poultry, to give me something to do during the long holidays. It was a grand paying game for me as long as it lasted, for I received a fixed price for eggs and chickens for the table and for the young chickens hatched. I soon discovered that cocks did not lay eggs, so they were the first to be condemned; I did not do the slaughtering. My reign over the chickens did not last long; I think my mother put a stop to it. She did not like me spending so much time in the chicken house, which abounded in fleas.

I had my own garden plot, which I attended to or neglected according to fancy. It was a pity my father did not take up gardening rather than farming.

During that summer there was an epidemic of boils, and father was very troubled with them, and so was I. When cub-hunting began, we used to get up very early and follow the hounds. Returning home one morning, my pony stumbled and I came off. The hounds and huntsmen were just behind, round a bend in the road. My father, not wishing them to see what had happened, bundled me quickly up into the saddle, and I, to help myself, put my hand on his shoulder, and my thumb happened to alight on a bad boil. Father jumped about the road execrating, but managed to mount his horse before we were seen.

Mother was ailing all that summer, and died in the autumn, soon after Fräulein had returned from Germany. One of her dying requests was that Fraulein should remain with us. Her death was a great blow to my father, as they were devotedly attached. My father used to tell us children that he fell in love with my mother at a children's party, when he was only four years of age. He managed to get possession of her handkerchief and always treasured it. He also told us of various other incidents in connection with their youth, which made me firmly believe that he could never love another woman.

My father had a long and serious illness – brain fever – after mother's death. Ellen was then just eighteen years of age – rather young to manage the household and also nurse her father. There were no trained nurses or nursing homes in those days. Ellen was by no means a born nurse, and she was too young and inexperienced for the careful day and night nursing my father needed. He was very "nervy," and one of her "crimes" was to rattle the spoon against the medicine glass. Eventually Fräulein took Ellen's place, and nursed my father most carefully day and night until he began to recover. I well remember seeing her crawling to her room one morning, looking tired and dazed and very pale. No doubt her good nursing saved my father's life.

While he was picking up strength, she, poor thing, became seriously ill, and I am afraid she got very scant attention or consideration from anybody unless it was from the servants. We children all got it into our heads that my father was going to marry her, and all joined forces to prevent that happening. What we did or said I cannot remember, but whatever it was it had the desired effect, for by the time Fräulein was up and about again, father had decided on his second marriage. He was married in London fifteen months after my mother's death. We four eldest children attended the wedding. We spent the night in London, with our old friends the Grays. Mrs. Charles Dickens was still living opposite their house, and we surreptitiously watched her from the front window as she frequently opened the front door to admit or dismiss her friends. Our London friends considered that such an unladylike proceeding was quite sufficient cause for her husband to refuse to live with her. We had to peep between the curtains very clandestinely, as that too was considered a great breach of etiquette in those days.

Fräulein left us soon after my father's second marriage, and then Pem and I walked every day to Dartford and back, he to a tutor and I to a girls' school, where he left me and called later for me, and we returned home together. Leaving the premises unaccompanied was one of the strictest prohibitions applied to the girls of our family.

My stepmother and I very soon fell out, the chief cause being, I think, dress. When my mother died, I was at an age when clothes were worn out and outgrown very quickly. Ellen was not provided very liberally with housekeeping money, and spent nothing on undergarments for me. When she handed over the reins of government to my stepmother, my wardrobe sadly needed replenishing.

My stepmother did provide some nightcaps, but they were so ugly that I did not wear them and have never worn any since. I do not think I was ever so fortunate as to get "new" clothes. Being one of the younger children and very small, I came in for the outgrown and cast-off garments of the elder ones. I had Pem's outgrown shoes, and tried hard to wear them thoroughly out by walking on the stoniest paths I could find. A dressmaker came to the house and worked with the head nurse at cutting down and making other dresses fit me. There were no "ready mades" in those days. The skirts were worn fairly long, and the drawers with frills or embroidery showed below. We always wore three petticoats: the first was of red flannel, the second of merino, and the top one was white, generally embroidered or trimmed with flounces. Most children wore bonnets, but my head would not fit a bonnet, so a Leghorn hat was made especially for me. The same hat did for winter and summer for many a year, with just a change of ribbon.

Before my mother died, crinolines were worn in Paris – probably it was shortly before the Prince Imperial was born. One of the last few walks I had with my mother was to make a call upon a young married woman, who showed her a crinoline she had just received from Paris. It was made of steel hoops and really resembled a round cage. The fashion was not generally adopted in England till quite two years later, and came at the time I was going to the girls' school in Dartford. My school fellows had them, I naturally wanted to be in the fashion, and as my stepmother did not provide me with one, I managed out of my scanty allowance to get yards of cane which I sewed into one of my petticoats. My first crinoline was not a success, for bits of cane would break loose and appear below my long dress at awkward times and places.

My father had a patent case in connection with crinolines, and as my elder brother was at King's College at that time, and he went up to London every day, he went to the Records Office to hunt up what he could find there that bore upon my father's patent case. During his "hunting" he raked up some very curious old deeds. One in particular I remember, drawn up in Queen Mary's reign, related to £30 a year for the burning of heretics. The fund had been increasing ever since. Probably the Charity Commissioners have dealt with it long ago.

I had a white beaver hat for riding. On the whole we were very well dressed during mother's lifetime, which made the contrast so galling afterwards.

There were no bathrooms at Bowman's Lodge; in fact, there was no water supply upstairs. All the water for the house was drawn from a well, a pony going round and round to work the pump. By this means a cistern was filled and a kitchen boiler. As there was a carpenter always employed on the place, he was ordered to make some wooden baths for us – they were like diminutive pig scalding tubs. The eldest "Miss Fooks" had one in her room curtained off, and there were several in other rooms in the house. When my stepmother came she wanted us to give up the baths, as she said it gave the servants too much work to carry the water upstairs for them. I would not submit, but Ellen did not seem to mind, as she was just about to be married. She was married a year after my father's second marriage. When I went to Tasmania with my father, he loved the comfort of the baths on board ship, and immediately on his return home he started to add bathrooms to the old house; but they were never completed. My stepmother boasted that she had never had a bath and had never drunk a glass of water.

In January 1858, when I was fourteen years of age, my brothers learned to skate. There were ponds on Dartford Heath, and they got up early in the morning and skated before breakfast by lantern light. I soon joined them, but all the help they gave me was to drag me to the middle of the pond and leave me to tumble about by myself.

I cannot remember where we got our skates from, unless we found them amongst the old lumber in the house. They were the sort of skates that screwed on to our boots. But soon I was presented with a lovely pair by one of my brother's friends, who had to ask permission of my father first if he might give them. They were a real joy to me, and I soon became an expert skater, but found out in later years, when skating in Germany (at Leipzig and Dresden) with Americans and Canadians, that I was not very efficient in comparison. No ladies skated in England when I learned, and I believe it was considered highly improper until some years later, when Princess Alexandra came over from Denmark to marry the then Prince of Wales. Skating then became all the rage, and Acme skates were worn, doing away largely with the old style of skates. My younger brother became too venturesome on his skates, and tried to achieve jumping, resulting in a broken leg which ended the skating for that winter.

While my brother was unable to get about, except on crutches, we were all invited to dine with the parents of my stepmother (my father was married to her on January 1st of that year). Pem being unable to go, I of course also stayed away to keep him company, so we were alone in the house except for the maid-servants. My brother was on the sofa in the lower dining-room, I sitting by his side, when the servants rushed in in great alarm and said there were burglars in the house. Of course they were too frightened to go and find out the cause of the noise they had heard, neither would they go to the cottages to fetch the groom and gardener. Pem and I had not heard any noise. I heated the poker red-hot. He on his crutches and I with the red-hot poker in one hand and a candlestick in the other went in search of the burglars. The candle gave a very poor light.

I must own to having felt a bit afraid. We searched every place where a robber could possibly hide. Last of all we went down to the semi-basement, where there were some huge bins in which the oats for the horses were kept. Pem, while I held up the lid, stirred the oats about with one of his crutches, but failed to find the burglars. By that time we had plucked up great courage, and one of us said, "Let us make the burglars laugh," and we set to work to spit into the oats. Nothing resulted, so we returned to the warm sitting-room and did our best to calm the fears of the servants. Daylight revealed the cause of the noise that had frightened the maids – a large chandelier had fallen in the upper dining-room.

Housebreaking was not so prevalent then as it had been some years previously. One winter nearly every sizable house was broken into excepting Bowman's Lodge. Whether Bowman's Lodge escaped owing to its being well known that my father kept loaded guns in the house and would have had no scruple in making use of them, or whether our luck was due to a light shining through the trees, I do not know. This light was given by a rushlight burning in a sort of lantern pierced with holes all night in the nursery bedroom.

There were no nightlights in those days as we now know them. Nightlights came into use about 1856. I remember my father had the patent business in connection with them and candles. Glycerine was then discovered as a byproduct and used for candle-making. A bottle of glycerine was sent to my mother to see if she would take it instead of the cod-liver oil which she so disliked, but unfortunately she did not long survive to take either. There can be few people living who remember rushlights. A very good account of them and their making is given in White's *Natural History of Selborne.*

At the age of sixteen I began to pay visits to relations. I found myself most unsuitably dressed and had to undergo the dreadful humiliation of being smartened up and supplied with necessaries. This happened once when I went to stay with an aunt who was married to a wellto-do Leeds merchant. On my arrival my aunt bustled into my room with her lady's maid for the latter to unpack my box and help me to dress. She told me to put on my best dress, as "eligibles" were coming to dine. My knowledge of society did not extend to an inkling of the word or its meaning, and I was also astonished that I was on no account to let it be known that I rode with the hounds. As soon as I was dressed, my aunt's stepdaughter came to take me to the drawing-room. I saw at once how different her dress was from mine, but she did not make me uncomfortable by scanning me. But my aunt's face when we entered the drawing-room was an awful picture! I was dressed in a very old-fashioned dress of figured silk with flounces up to the waist. Probably it was an old dress of my mother's. Flounces had been out of fashion for years. Quite plain silk dresses were then worn. My diminutive form must really have looked grotesque. Whatever made the man who took me in to dinner talk about hunting and ask me if I hunted, I cannot think, but we were near enough to my aunt for her to hear, and her look made me feel hot all over and quite unable to utter a word. I do not remember any further conversation with that eligible.

The next morning my aunt came into my room with patterns of material for a dress, and we drove into Leeds, where she set me up with some very nice things, especially a becoming hat. Hats had just then come into fashion for girls. When I returned home, my father gave me an allowance of £20 per annum for dress – quite inadequate, as the effect of the American war was still felt. Cotton longcloth was 1s. 4d. a yard, and very poor stuff even at that price. I was very jealous of some of my London girlfriends, who had £100 per annum for pin-money.

Crinolines were worn generally then. Mine never extended over three yards in circumference, but a tall friend had one that measured seven yards when crinolines were at the height of that ridiculous fashion. I took care not to go away on a visit again till I was properly equipped. A decent habit and riding gloves ran off with nearly all my first quarter's allowance.

Amongst our Dartford friends were the Keymers, who lived in a large house near the church. My father and Mr. Keymer were old acquaintances and had much in common. They were of the same political opinions and took great interest in the local Ragged School, where they often got up lectures, to some of which I went. I remember my father gave a lecture there on "Law." I do not suppose the children were at all interested. I certainly was not. I thought it very dry. The Keymers had several literary relations and friends. The Blanchards, the Jerrolds (William Jerrold, son of Douglas Jerrold), and Sir John Lubbock often visited their house. Some of these friends also lectured at the Ragged School. The lecture I remember best was given by Augustus Mayhew on "Rats."

Laura Keymer became my bosom friend, the only real girlfriend I ever had. She was four years my senior, and married, a few years after we became acquainted, Mr. Cosmo Monkhouse, who later was well known as an art critic. Laura had artistic tastes, and although untaught she could draw from nature fairly well. She tried to instruct me, but I proved a hopeless pupil. The lessons she gave me were in the garden of her home, where there was a fair-sized piece of water on which was a boat. The boat had more attractions for me than the brush and palette.

The winter after we became acquainted was very severe, and the pond in her garden was frozen over. Our brothers went up to London, hoping to get some skating on Regent's Canal, but the ice was not safe, and seven over-venturesome skaters were drowned. Laura and I thought the ice on the pond would bear us if we did not keep together, so a long plank was placed by the gardener across the pond, and we each had a portion of the ice to skate on. My piece was soon so cracked and bent so ominously that I reluctantly gave up. My friend called out, "Do go on, as I want to make a sketch of the bending ice." I complied, but, alas! the ice broke and I went head first into the water. Fortunately I was near the bank, where the water was not deep enough to drown me. The gardener came to the rescue with a rake and drew me out. It was a lesson never to go skating unless the ice was perfectly safe.

My friend dressed me up in her clothes and her mother gave me a hot drink; then I walked home. I told my father nothing about the accident. I happened to have my best dress on when I got the ducking. It was a blue and white checked silk made with two bodices, one high and one low, so as to serve as an evening or afternoon dress. It was ruined. My father often asked what had become of it. It was a strange dress to go skating in, but probably I was going to stay the evening with the Keymer's, and my father would call in for me, as was his habit, on his return from town.

Fraulein, who had left after my father's marriage, returned about this time to teach my two younger sisters. I did not spend much time in the schoolroom, but Fräulein and I translated Shakespeare's Julius Caesar into German. During her absence she had been learning Italian, and imparted a smattering to me. She and I got on in quite a friendly way together, but she hated my stepmother in true German style. I think the hate was reciprocated.

As I was fully determined not to visit again without being suitably dressed, I had to devise a way out of the difficulty. My friend Laura besides being very artistic, was clever with her needle, and helped me to turn my

£20 allowance to good account. I also ran up a bill at the local linen-draper's shop to pay when I came of age. I was not aware at the time that my father was responsible for my debts.

My stepmother was always a sort of thorn in the flesh, but although we suffered at her hands she had many a reason to feel hurt with us. My parents liked to see my elder brother and sister at the head and foot of the table, and they sat together at the side. Before my father married again he explained to his future wife that he wished this custom to remain unaltered. It would have been wiser if she had objected then than to resent it after their marriage. It was not until Ellen's marriage that my stepmother got her rights, and afterwards she always sat at one end of the table. Whatever her shortcomings were, I always try to remember her as I saw her once having a hearty laugh.

When I was returning from my second trip to New Zealand, I received a letter from my brother at Port Said in which he said that our stepmother had met with a carriage accident and been "knocked into a cocked hat."

It was my stepmother's habit when out driving to send the groom to execute commissions, so leaving the horse unattended. She was afraid of horses, yet she persisted in running the risk of the horse bolting. That is what happened on this occasion. "Jim," the horse, took fright at something or other and made off; hence the accident. My father met me as soon as I landed in England and begged me to take the place of my sister Ellen, who had been nursing and keeping house for our stepmother and was anxious to get home to her own domestic duties. I went to look after my stepmother. She ought to have had a nurse, as she required constant attention. She was up and about, but if she tried to walk alone she tottered and fell continually. Soon after my arrival she expressed a wish to see the clothes she was wearing at the time of the accident. Ellen had told me she had been putting off the evil hour on account of not liking to tell our stepmother what had become of her best bonnet.

The garments were produced – most of them had been consigned to the wash-tub. She lamented long and loudly over the ruin of her velvet jacket. At the time of the accident a doctor who lived close by attended to her. He had cut the velvet jacket instead of unpicking the seam. I doubt if she would have enjoyed the seam being unpicked, as her arm was broken, besides other damage. She missed her best bonnet and asked what had become of it. I burst out laughing, and she could not help laughing too when I explained that the doctor had taken her bonnet for her to be sick in! I suppose he thought a well-conducted matron could not be sick without something to be sick in.

"Jim" was a particular friend of mine – I had brought him from Wales a few years previous to the accident. My father had a farm in Wales, and we went there sometimes during the long vacation. He kept several horses there. Amongst them was "Jim", which my father thought would make a suitable horse for my stepmother's brougham, and he deputed me to go into Wales and bring the horse back with me. I went by train to Dolgellau. It was late in November. The bailiff met me and drove me to the farm. My father had written previously to the bailiff to feed the horse up and make him fit for the journey. "Jim" was very much of a mixture as regards colour – sorrel predominated, and he was in a very rough condition with his winter coat.

When I set out from the farm, the bailiff showed me a short cut to the main road to Shrewsbury through the Cader Passes. I carried a bag of oatmeal to put in his water whenever he drank, and fed him up well with feeds of corn on the road. I got very much more corn for my money at small country inns than in the towns. I intended to ride forty miles a day on the average, but by the time I got to Wellington, "Jim" was off his feed and, in fact, done. An ostler told me that the horse must have a rest, so I decided the rest should be in the train and sent him on by train to Oxford, where I arrived before "Jim." As I was in my riding habit and rather travel stained, I called on a cousin there, and she, being about the same size as myself, was able to rig me out in suitable attire.

When I returned to the station for "Jim," a few undergraduates were hanging around and, seeing me go with a porter to take him out of the horse-box, were led by curiosity to follow; but when they saw "Jim," with his shaggy, unkempt coat, the look of disgust on their faces was really amusing. Evidently they were no judges of horses or they would have seen that under that coat was a good animal. The next day I rode "Jim" to London, and found good stables in the neighbourhood where my brother lived, with whom I spent the night. "Jim's" rough and uncouth appearance and remarkable colour attracted the attention of the street boys, who fairly mobbed me. "Jim" was terrified, never having been in a crowd and traffic before.

To avoid the unpleasant attentions of the boys, I was obliged to make a very early start next day. It was a frosty morning and the roads very slippery. At the entrance to Hyde Park "Jim" and I came under the notice of a policeman. I was afraid of trouble, for "Jim" was a little girth galled; but when he heard I had brought him all the way from Wales and was only going to ride him to the neighbourhood of Dartford, he let me pass. Through the Park, to avoid the slippery part of the road, I had to ride close to the footpath, where a gentleman was taking his early constitutional. The horse, seemingly proud of being in such fashionable quarters, cocked up his bobbed tail, threw up his head, and neighed lustily, cutting altogether a ludicrous figure. At Eltham I called on my sister Edith, who was staying there. When she saw "Jim" and me, she exclaimed, "I think this is the pluckiest thing you have ever done." About eight miles farther brought me to Bowman's Lodge, where my father was waiting for us at the gate. "Jim" was soon clipped, groomed, and brought into good condition.

I have digressed a little. I must now return to the time of the Indian Mutiny. We had many relations in India. My father was one of seventeen children to grow up, and most of his brothers and sisters had been provided for by an uncle by marriage, Sir George Larpent, who was a director of the East India Company. My father had commenced his early career as a clerk in the East India Company's Office, probably a post procured for him by his uncle. He was there at the same time as Charles Lamb, but I could never get my father to tell me much about him beyond the fact that he, my father, was his junior.

Two of my father's younger brothers were in the East India Company's army. Several of his sisters went out to India in couples, always provided with pink bonnets! They all married with the exception of one, and she on her return home married a Leeds merchant.

One of my father's sisters was killed during the Mutiny. She was married to a Colonel Ewart, and they were stationed at Cawnpore when the Mutiny broke out. Colonel Ewart was wounded in the trenches, and when Cawnpore was taken by Nana Sahib, he had to be carried in a litter, with his wife, with a nurse and baby, following on foot. They were all massacred by the bearers before arriving at the banks of the Ganges. It was thought for some time that the ayah had escaped with the baby, but search was made in vain. They had another child who had been left in England when they went to India, and he is still living and settled in Eastbourne. The last letters received from Cawnpore were from my aunt, and I think there is mention of them in Trevelyan's History of Cawnpore.

During the mutiny there were very many narrow escapes. Another aunt and her family had decided to make their escape by a certain road when some friendly natives persuaded them to take another, which advice it was as well they took; otherwise they would have been murdered.

Colonel Ewart was considered a very good chess player, and when I was between the age of seven and eight I played a game of chess with him and nearly beat him, for he went to sleep over the game!

Laura's husband, Cosmo Monkhouse, was first cousin to that solitary man, Mr. Delafosse, who escaped from Cawnpore, and at one time of my life I met many of his relations. I think I met the hero of Cawnpore himself. He managed to escape by getting to the banks of the Ganges. Being a strong swimmer, he crossed the Ganges by diving and swimming alternately, and then crawled to a temple. There he was laid up ill for a long time, and was nursed and tended by a native woman. It was some while before his relations in England knew that he had made his escape and that he was alive and well.

I distinctly remember the great Tooley Street fire. I was in London when it broke out, and it continued to burn for a week or more. We could see the glow in the sky from Bowman's Lodge, fifteen miles away.

* * * * *

When in my seventeenth year, I went to stay with my uncle at Thame, twelve miles from Oxford. As I have recounted on an earlier page of these recollections, my uncle was head master of Thame Grammar School. He was a keen fisherman, and he fished in the River Darenth; he was also a regular society man and very popular wherever he went. He was chaplain to Lady Wenman of Thame Park.

My uncle was very fond of walking, and often walked to Oxford and stayed there with his wife's relations. One day his eldest daughter and I started to walk to Oxford with him, but she got tired and turned back. My uncle took me on, and my cousin sent me the necessary attire by coach (there was no train then).

We spent a few days in Oxford. Of course I was taken to see all the sights, but what pleased me most was the chapel music. I remember being perfectly thrilled on hearing an anthem in the chapel of Christ Church College. It was the first anthem I had ever heard. It was strange that my father should have taken me as a child to an Italian Opera but never to the Temple Church, although he was then a member of the Middle Temple.

Soon after our walk back to Thame, my uncle and aunt and his daughters and I were invited to stay at Winchendon Priory, then owned by Mr. Bernard (later Sir Thomas). Mr. Bernard was a great lover of music – he played the 'cello, but was not a very fine performer. My uncle was a thorough musician – he played the violin. The first violin was the organist from Aylesbury, Herr Deichmann, who was staying in the house as a paid guest. He later became musical director of the Albert Hall Orchestra. His portrait used to hang in the Albert Hall, and probably does still. We had music from morning to night, just a break for meals and a walk in the afternoon. I, being able to speak German, usually walked with Herr Deichmann. My visit was a musical education to me, which I greatly appreciated. Every evening there was a dinner party, conspicuous among the guests being Archdeacon and Mrs. Bickersteth. Mrs. Bickersteth was much older than her husband. She was the first specimen of a painted lady I had ever seen, and I was so puzzled at what appeared to be a youngish head on a very wrinkled neck! There was a story current that a butler once announced the Archdeacon and his wife as "The Archdeacon and Venerable Mrs. Biekersteth."

In spite of having what is now called "a good time" at Thame, I grew homesick and wrote to my father to send for me or fetch me home. I said unless he did, and very soon, I should walk home! Upon which threat my father sent my brother Pem to fetch me. We had to take the coach to Aylesbury, as that was the nearest station to Thame. I often visited my uncle again. His two elder daughters got married, and the third one, my age, died; so my uncle was glad to have me to accompany him on his walks. My aunt was not strong, and she did not like walking.

I sometimes accompanied my uncle on Sunday mornings, when he held the service in Thame Park chapel. He always had lunch after the service with Lady Wenman, and when any member of his family was with him, he or she was always asked in to luncheon too. I dreaded the ordeal; Lady Wenman was such a formidable and stiff old lady.

When I was nineteen years of age I was staying at Thame just before Commemoration time at Oxford. Three young Oxfordians, friends of my brother, came over to Thame one Sunday and enquired of me whether I would be in Oxford for Commemoration week. Without asking my uncle, I told them I had no idea of being present, and they said in that case they would not stay up themselves.

When Commemoration time came, my uncle decided to go to Oxford to see what was going on. Directly we arrived, a cousin at Christ Church College invited us to lunch with him and several of his young men friends. He gave me a ticket for the Christ Church Ball and instructed his friends to look after me. He could not go to the Ball himself, as I had told him I should not be at the Commemoration, and he had given notice that he was going down. My uncle did not go to the Ball, but found me a chaperone with a daughter who was very smartly dressed. She scanned me up and down and made me feel rather in the shade, as I was only dressed in a very simple grenadine muslin.

One of my cousin's friends sought me for the first dance, which in those days was always a quadrille. He said, "We will go and dance in the Duke's set." After the dance, and when I was sitting by my chaperone, a steward came up and asked my name, and introduced the Duke of Hamilton, who put his name on my card for a round dance and, when that dance was over, for others, including the last of all, which was encored.

After the encore, soup was served and then the Duke took me back to the ballroom, but there was no chaperone,

Studio portrait of the author as a young woman aged 22, around 1866.

only my wrap. The Duke soon found my chaperone's carriage, with her and her daughter seated inside, none too amiable at what they considered my "luck." The Duke offered to send me tickets for the Freemasons' Ball the following night, but I refused and would not give him my address, bearing in mind that my father had prohibited my receiving presents from men and the Duke was "nubbut a mon arter all," as the Yorkshireman said when he saw a judge in the procession when the Assizes were held at Leeds for the first time. On that occasion my elder brother held his first brief (about Soup). But the Duke danced well, and I suppose I did too.

Before going to the Ball, my uncle had jokingly said, "Mind you dance with the Duke." At breakfast next morning he said, "And how did the Duke dance?" "Splendidly," I replied. My uncle was much astonished, and was quite angry with me for having refused tickets for the Masonic Ball, saying he would have chaperoned me himself sooner than I should not have gone, adding that at Commemoration time it was quite etiquette to receive tickets from comparative strangers. I plead guilty to having nourished a hope that the Duke would find out my address and that tickets for the Freemasons' Ball would arrive, but nothing so romantic and fairy-tale like happened.

Only once again did I set eyes on the Duke of Hamilton. It was at the Croydon races. My husband and I went to them on our return from our honeymoon. My husband left me in the grand stand. From there, on looking down to the betting ring, I saw the Duke, surrounded by whom I suppose were betting men and looking quite different from when I danced with him at the Commemoration Ball. My uncle was a very welcome guest wherever he went, and we thoroughly "did" Commemoration week, it being for me "the time of my life."

The Crystal Palace had become the centre of amusement. There was a promenade where friends met. Manns's concerts were very popular; they were the first concerts where silence had to be observed. Manns did a great deal for the musical world. He brought forward much talent that but for him would not have been recognised.

The first automaton I remember being exhibited in London was the anthropoglossis at the Egyptian Hall. It was just a bust that talked. Probably it was only ventriloquism. Later there was an automaton chess player at the Crystal Palace with which I played and was beaten. The chessmen were all the same height, which was baulking when one was not accustomed to it.

In after years I was with my father at Maskelyne and Cooke's entertainment at Queen's Hall. We went on to the platform to play whist with the automaton "Psycho." Father cut in with Psycho, I with a stranger from the audience. He and I won. Father was not a good whist player. After the game was finished, Mr. Maskelyne asked me to shake hands with my opponent Psycho, which I did, but the sensation was very unpleasant. I tried to pull my hand away, and it felt like pulling a lot of wires till Mr. Maskelyne said, "Let go, Psycho." He immediately released my hand.

My father made a thorough examination of Psycho. After the cards were dealt, he asked if he might again examine the automaton. Mr. Maskelyne said, "Yes, provided you do not look at your partner's hand." Father passed his stick all round Psycho and thoroughly examined him, but was fairly puzzled. I am credited with being the only lady who ever beat Psycho at whist.

Advertisement for the Psycho automaton.

About the year 1862 an uncle and aunt, who were staying in London getting outfits for themselves and their children before returning to India, asked me to stay with them to accompany my uncle sightseeing. My aunt was too occupied shopping and looking after the children, and in indifferent health at the time, so felt herself unable to undertake any extra exertion.

I had never been to a theatre and only twice to an opera. I think we went to a theatre every night, but I was not impressed with anything I heard or saw except a play called *Leah* and Miss Bateman's acting. On our return from the theatre, my aunt always had an oyster supper ready for us and entertained us with her adventures shopping in Westbourne Grove, and told us of the wonderful bargains she got at an insignificant shop kept by a man called Whiteley. Ready hemmed pocket handkerchiefs were what particularly impressed her. Every article in the window was priced distinctly and at a low sum, quite a novelty then.

It was some time before any other shop followed Whiteley's example of ticketing their goods, and for still longer it was considered very *infra dig.* to deal at shops that had the price written up or to ask the price before purchasing.

Some fourteen or fifteen years later, when I returned from New Zealand, Whiteley's had become a large and important shop. It was said that Mrs. Whiteley's skill in dressmaking was the making of her husband's business. My younger sister had recently purchased a satin evening dress there, and was enthusiastic regarding the fit and style.

CHAPTER III

PIONEER IN NEW ZEALAND FROM 1867

I HAVE visited the Antipodes five times; my first journey there was with my husband in 1867. We, my fiancé and I, had our inclinations for travelling fanned when we went to Gravesend to see a cousin off in one of the first three steamers that went out to New Zealand and eventually plied between Panama and New Zealand. The comforts of the steamer appeared most luxurious to us then. My fiancé asked me if I would like to go out too. As my favourite brother, Pem, was there, and I was longing to see him and also was keen to travel and see the world, I readily acquiesced.

After we were married in February 1867 and all necessary arrangements made, we took passage in a West Indian mail packet to the West Indies. We were to have changed steamers at St. Thomas and go on to Colon, but yellow fever raged at St. Thomas, so we went on to Peter

Island, one of the Virgin group, the beauties of which are fully described in Kingsley's 'At Last'.

From Peter Island we went to Colon, then a most horrible place – mosquitoes of the worst description. The heat was truly awful. I have no recollection of being able to obtain any ice. Cocktails and corpse revivers did not cool us.

The railway line crossing the Isthmus to Panama had not long been finished. It was said that every sleeper had cost a life. The forty miles over the Isthmus took four hours in a funny little train which stopped for wood for fuel as required. There were large stacks of wood at intervals along the line.

At Panama the heat was so great that it was not safe to venture out during the day, and at night we and our fellow passengers were cautioned, and told we should be robbed and murdered if we went out of doors. We were held up at Panama for some days on account of the revolution which was then raging in Mexico. All the coal-heavers had gone up there to fight, and the tragedy of the execution of Maximilian took place then.

The journey on to New Zealand was not eventful except for a fire on board and a stop at Pitcairn Island to deliver a harmonium and other things sent by Queen Victoria to the descendants of the mutineers of the Bounty. We stood off for two hours, but it was too rough to land, or for the natives to come off in their boats, so the inhabitants were obliged to wait for their gifts from the Queen till the return journey of the steamer.

At Wellington, then as now the seat of Government, we found the town very full of Maoris – unusually full so I was told, owing to land cases being tried in the courts.

We saw a large boat full of Maoris set sail to the Chatham Islands, where the New Zealand convict station was, to visit a convict, Ti-Cooti by name, who was there. He managed to escape in that boat and landed in Poverty Bay, where soon afterwards a massacre took place – he was in all probability the ringleader. All the settlers were killed with the exception of one man and a boy. The boy escaped to the bush near his parents' house. As soon as he heard the Maoris retreating, he returned to the house to look for his mother. He found her dreadfully wounded, but still alive. He collected eggs to leave by her side and started off for the nearest settlement to get help. On the way he heard tramping of feet and hid in the bush again, but the "fright" this time turned out to be military settlers coming to the relief of Poverty Bay, but alas! too late to save the poor boy's mother. She lingered for some days, but died from her wounds and the shock. The boy came to live with his relations near to our home. He may be alive still; if so, I would very much like to meet him.

There were many building plots in the middle of Wellington to be bought for about £20. I wanted to buy one with part of £30 my father-inlaw had given me on leaving England to buy a watch, which I really did not need. My husband did not approve of the idea of purchasing a plot of ground, so the £30 went in buying our first milch cow and the dairy utensils. We had our first introduction to earthquakes while in Wellington – there were no less than three during our short stay.

As our destination was Canterbury, we embarked in a coastal steamer at Wellington which took us to Lyttelton, the port for Christchurch. We drove to Christchurch; some of the passengers walked over the Port Hills, as in those days there was no railway. At Christchurch we were met by a cousin of my father's, a retired Indian Civil Servant, Mr. Cracroft Wilson, later knighted for his services. He had held the position of Judge and Sessions Judge of Moradabad, and when the Mutiny broke out he was appointed Commissioner on special duty. In his narrative of 'Events Attending the Outbreak of Disturbances', which was written at the express command of the Governor General, Lord Canning, he gives a very graphic account of the Mutiny as he saw it.

When Mr. Cracroft Wilson left India, he settled in New Zealand instead of returning to England. He had brought his Indian servants, some sheep, and a stallion with him. While his house was being built, he and his wife lived in a mud "whare." He was one of the earliest settlers and had taken up a great deal of land. He had three "runs" – two sheep runs and one cattle run – and also the land lying between his dwelling and the boundary of Christchurch, mostly swamp land. It is now built over and is very valuable. Canterbury in the early days was called "the gentleman's Colony." Most of the early Colonists were of the good old families from the West of England.

During the three months we lived with my father's cousin, I was longing to be in the swim of all the gaiety that was going on – balls, theatres, and much visiting – but neuralgia had got hold of me and I was quite unfit to enjoy anything.

Mr. Cracroft Wilson acted as my trustee, and was really more like a father to me than my own father. His wife was kindness itself, giving me what nursing I required.

The family consisted of Mr. and Mrs. Cracroft Wilson, a son, retired from the army, with his wife and three children. They had English servants in the house; the native servants he had brought from India had their own huts at a little distance from the house.

Most of the native servants married Maori women.

Mr. Cracroft Wilson was an M.P, which took him to Wellington during session, and public duties in Christchurch engaged a good deal of his time. He was at home for the three months we were with them, but hard at work in the swamp. His son was often at the cattle station eighty miles south, and took my husband with him to draft and shift cattle, which, being nearly wild, was sport to his liking. Had our career been successful in New Zealand, it would have been owing to these kind relations of mine.

When we arrived in New Zealand, no more Government land was available or suitable for a "run," so we had to become freeholders. At the end of three months we found a beautiful freehold about fifty miles from Christchurch up the gorge of the river Wiapara. It was already fenced, and so far as New Zealand houses went, it had a good house built of limestone. The stone had been quarried from a ridge of limestone which ran through the property. One great drawback was that there was no proper road leading to the house. The former owner had spent £300 in making a way up three miles of the river bed, crossing and recrossing and avoiding quicksands, all of which work was washed away by a flood just after we took possession. Such a flood the Maoris said they had not seen for fifty years.

My husband had been so greatly complimented on the way he wielded the stock whip when he was on the Cracroft Wilson's cattle station that he insisted on keeping cattle contrary to all advice, as our land and the neighbourhood was distinctly a sheep country. A neighbouring run was never free from "scab." The laws relating to scab were very severe, and they probably so alarmed my husband that that was another reason why he insisted on keeping cattle.

The purchase of our property, and £100 for only absolutely necessary furniture, which we had great difficulty in getting up country, ran away with all our capital. My husband applied to his father for more and several times more, and on that we lived. The cattle were not a paying proposition, and were eventually sold with the increase for less than we gave for them. My husband, realising that no living was to be made simply from the increase of the cattle, decided that we must start a dairy. I was to try my hand at cheese-making, to test whether the pasture was good enough to make dairying pay. Ten halfwild heifers were broken in. The cheese was quite a success, but on turning it daily in the making its shape was altered. The "vat" I made it in was half an old brandy keg with gimlet holes for drainage. When the cheese was made, I did not like to see the milk from the ten cows thrown away, so I obtained a keg and decided to make butter and salt it down. First-rate butter was then selling at 4½d. a pound; at the same time most delicious honey was only fetching 2½d. a pound. A movement was afoot to send salt butter to England. Mine went with the first consignment, but the export plan did not answer. My butter fetched 6½d. a pound. The storekeeper told me it ranked with the best that was sent in.

When those ten cows and tame milk cows were in milk, my maid, a German girl – an excellent worker – asked for her holiday; at the same time my husband must needs give the man who did the milking his holiday, intending to do the man's work himself. Not a bit of it! So the milking devolved on me, and thankful I was that I had learned to milk when a small child. The cows had to be driven into a stockyard and roped – at that time the yard was deep in mud. One cow in particular greatly objected to being roped, and she also objected to women. My husband's roping was not very successful, and she got her head free and looked round at me with such a wicked glare in her eye. Then she managed to get a leg loose and put it into the milk pail; immediately her expression changed to one of great satisfaction.

While waiting for more capital from home our land was stocked with half-wild lean cattle from Mr. Cracroft Wilson's "run" to fatten on our good pasture. When the money arrived my husband bought young heifers, thinking that the increase would provide an income on which we could live. The price of stock cattle and sheep went down and down; "run" holders with mortgaged "runs" were ruined, the banks being obliged to sell them up. Broken-mouthed ewes could be bought for 6d. a head. The owner of a sheep "run" which nearly surrounded our freehold had a copper in which 500 sheep were boiled down at a time, just for the fat and skins. The liquor was used for manuring his home paddocks, but it was rather too strong and caused the death of several valuable horses.

History was repeating itself! As the master did not work, the man was slack. My husband could not fall into Colonial ways; roughing it was not to his taste. He had grand opportunities, but never believed in the future of New Zealand. He was a pessimist. I am an optimist, and drew a vivid mental picture of the then worthless land being cultivated and covered with flourishing farms. My husband did not take to work; he had not been brought up to it, and I suppose was too old to learn. He was a thorough sportsman, hunted and shot, and was a good judge of cattle. He wanted bits and bridles, girths and harness, kept as in England. It was not sufficient for his bits to be kept in a strong solution of soda water when not in use and simply wiped over when wanted. He wished them to have a first-rate shine; but there was no time for polishing with such a small staff as we kept. He also clung to the white girths as then used in England instead of adopting the popular New Zealand girth made of hide.

Where we lived we had plenty of sport wild boar hunting. Wild pigs were very plentiful in the surrounding mountains. Eeling after dark was another sport we indulged in. There were three kinds of wild duck: the Paradise duck, which was large and very wild; a blue duck, which was rather rare; and another, very like our wild duck, also very wild and which proved very tough when cooked.

There was also a large wild pigeon, but that was scarce. A wingless bird, called the weka[3], was very plentiful; its plumage was something like a pheasant's, but more dingy. He was a very lively bird at night, and would keep us awake with his noisy squawking. He was a terrible thief and very daring. If you were to sit still in the tussock grass, soon several would appear and peck at the eyelets of your boots!

My husband nearly lost a valuable watch through their thieving propensities. He left his watch in the pocket of his waistcoat, which he had taken off and thrown on the ground. When he went to put on his waistcoat again he found the watch had been taken. Fortunately, after a good hunt, we found it in the tussocks. Evidently a weka was trying to make off with it.

---

3. A endemic brown, flightless bird the size of a chicken

When we went for picnics we always had to hang our nosebags in a tree out of reach of the weka. On one occasion I hid a small bottle of whisky on the ground. I had tied some white kid over the neck of the bottle, but a thieving weka managed to pull out the cork. The whisky drinkers of the party thought it was a practical joke on my part, but I was quite innocent.

Wekas were not edible. Maoris boiled them down for their oil. We had a small pet dog who would kill wekas, which was very useful, for we used the dead weka as a trap for hawks. When a hawk had pecked a hole in the dead weka, we inserted strychnine. The hawks returned to their feast, and we would pick them up shortly after quite dead on the brink of a lagoon, where they had gone to drink, owing to their great thirst from the strychnine. These hawks were very large and great enemies to our chickens.

A small sparrow hawk was really a much worse enemy, but fortunately scarce. Once one alighted amongst our chickens while they were being fed and struck left and right, then made for the eyes of the man who was trying to drive it away. We were standing outside our house waiting for the man to bring up a horse for a departing guest, and my husband, seeing what was going on, fetched his gun and shot the hawk, but not before it had killed six chickens.

There were very few song-birds in the bush. The bell-bird had rather a mournful note. The tui, or parson bird, was a great treat when he elected to sing. In the bush was also a dingy reddish parrot which made its appearance in public when the flax was in blossom for the sake of the honey. I tried one in the stew-pot once, but it was not nice. There were also little green parakeets, but they did not often show themselves. We brought a brace of pheasants from Auckland, hoping they would increase, but very shortly after we turned them out, one was found dead, and nothing was ever seen or heard of the other. Shortly before leaving New Zealand, I heard a bird's call which strongly resembled a sound I had heard in England; my husband recognised it as the partridge call. We found the nest later, but they too were accounted for by the wekas.

Owing to the weka, we were obliged to take all the turkey eggs until the hen had finished laying, only leaving a nest-egg. When her eggs were returned to her, she never left her nest till the chicks were all hatched. The turkeys were able to defend their young from the hawks in a marvellous manner. As soon as the young were hatched, the turkey vanished with them, and they lived in the tussock grass on seeds, lizards, and grasshoppers. Just before winter set in they found their way back to the house, fat and well nourished. The first money we ever made was on the surplus turkeys we could not eat ourselves and sold to the manager of the nearest accommodation house at 7½d. a pound. Wild pig was not nice to eat, not at all like pork. Little pigs when caught were easily tamed, but they did not pay, as they took so long to fatten.

Beer was not much drunk in the early days of the Colony. The only brewery I heard of had failed – imported bottled beer and stout were to be had at a price. The usual drinks at public houses were brandy and whisky, and those probably much adulterated. My husband knew how to brew, as the servants' and workmen's beer was still being brewed at his father's home when we left for New Zealand, and with our first consignment of stores he ordered malt and dried hops. Hops were then not grown in the Colony or barley malted; but, notwithstanding, my husband did not tackle the job of brewing. The malt lay in the store for about a year and got full of maggots. At that time I had a servant who knew how to brew, and, instigated by her, during a few days' absence of my husband, we decided to try our skill at brewing. We used the same sort of yeast we made for our bread. I have forgotten the ingredients, but to keep it going neighbours exchanged their stock from time to time. Often the bottle burst in my husband's pocket when he was bringing it home on horseback.

Well, to return to our brewing. I began by picking the maggots out of the malt, but found it a hopeless task, so we just tipped them with the malt into the copper of boiling water. When my husband returned the beer was in the cask and working. When drawn it was not very palatable and was of a very dark colour, and I think kept young men neighbours away who were in the habit of looking in at all hours, as I gave it to them instead of the whisky they were accustomed to get. The saying went round in the neighbourhood, "Have you tasted Homewood's swipes?" When that brew was exhausted, my husband brewed proper beer minus maggots.

Candles we made in a mould. This was comparatively easy work, and when we changed from keeping cattle to sheep, our good pasture made our sheep so fat that it increased our supply of candles to such a degree that I was contemplating making soap when we left. Vinegar I made from a vinegar plant, but I forget the ingredients of the mixture required for it to grow in. The vinegar plant grows very rapidly and soon spreads over the mixture in the jar, and when ripe there is another plant under the parent one, so vinegar becomes a very cheap item in housekeeping. As pickles were much in request on account of the everlasting diet of mutton, and that in hot weather generally partaken of cold, vinegar was very useful. Some of my friends used honey in the place of sugar, as sugar was then more than double the price of honey, but we never kept bees.

The only approach to our house for the last three miles or so was a sort of sheep track on the mountain high above and overlooking the lovely river. We had the track widened and a shed built for our trap on the plain under a rock three miles from the house. We were seventeen miles from the post office and store. The daughter of a shepherd living near was my first maid. She was only fifteen years of age, but really a wonder. We kept one man, but little essential work seemed to get done. I tried to dig in order to make a garden, so that we could grow our own vegetables and flowers, but the virgin soil was beyond my powers. Our man made short work of the digging, and I soon had a most prolific garden. When it was time to "dig" potatoes, my husband said he would undertake the job.

We started off for the garden, which was a good distance from the house, he to dig and I to pick up; but very soon he was leaning against the gate with a pipe in his mouth and I was digging and picking up too. That was a sample of how the work was done on our lovely property.

Our nearest neighbours were Scottish shepherds. My husband soon made their acquaintance, and without consulting me had accepted an invitation to dine with one, a bachelor, about two miles away. I did not like the idea at all, but we went and had an excellent dinner, a beautifully cooked leg of mutton straight out of a camp oven, tea and a beaten-up egg tabirdken in the place of milk, whisky for my husband and port wine for myself. Soon I had another shock. My husband invited the proprietor of the nearest accommodation house, about seventeen miles distant, and his wife. I was silly enough to shed tears, and my husband regretted having asked them over; but when the time came I really enjoyed their visit. My husband took Mr. Paget round the estate, and Mrs. Paget gave me much useful, kind, and motherly advice. Those incidents and a few similar ones soon knocked all class pride out of my silly head.

Several nice families lived within riding distance. On Sundays we never knew how many had to be prepared for. From our house we could see to the end of the three mile gorge and were able to count the horses winding round the bridle path. Once a sheep had to be quickly killed, as we only had a turkey for dinner. The chops cut off that sheep were a bit tough.

Our house was not quite at the end of civilisation. There were two stations ("runs") beyond us, so our house was a place of call and rest to the owners as they came past. To the farthest off of these "runs" came a bride shortly after we had settled. She had not left her fads and fancies behind and imagined she could not eat mutton. Mutton was practically the only meat to be had, as no poultry had been kept on her husband's "run."

That poor bride's chief diet was wild pig, which had to be hunted and killed in the neighbourhood. It was not long before she discovered that she could eat mutton. Mutton was very excellent in those days, as the Merino sheep had not been crossed with the larger and coarser breeds.

How I loved the life, the freedom, the hospitality, the beautiful scenery, exploring the creeks and gullies. Those expeditions were glorious. Sometimes I went alone, sometimes with children who stayed with us, and sometimes with the Government geologist. A Government geologist's appointment was easy to get, as in those days a great deal of knowledge of the subject was not considered necessary. Dr. von Haast spent much time with us to study the features of the country around. But for the Great War the whole countryside would have been exploited long since. In fact, all plans were made for a deputation to go out from England in 1914 to explore and report upon the district, the members of which were to have stayed with the owners of our old house. They also invited me to stay at the same time, which would have been a great delight to me, but the war broke out, which frustrated all the plans, and so far as I know nothing has been done since. I feel sure I should have had my invitation renewed had the deputation gone out.

Floods often dislodged huge boulders from the high cliffs of one of our creeks. In those creeks were often found buried the antediluvian fossil remains of saurians. I loved exploring with Dr. von Haast and other guests interested in research. A huge head of a saurian which we found was packed on our pack saddle and sent to Lyttelton to be shipped to England for the British Museum. The vessel, which I think was the *Matoaka*, was lost with all hands. On board were some friends of ours from Christchurch, and also a man we knew who was taking petrifactions and sundry other curios home to my father-in-law.

The only shirts and collars my husband took out with him were of white linen. Up country such things were never seen, much less worn. There was nobody who knew how to get them "up." I tried in vain to starch and iron them, and in spite of lessons from Mrs. von Haast while she was staying with us, I was very far from successful. I wrote to his mother and asked her to send him some coloured flannel shirts, but she sent out white ones made of flannel, which shrank so much in the wash that they were soon quite useless. Necessity being the mother of invention, I soon found out the way to make some coloured flannel shirts. Linen collars up country were quite dispensed with. I also made my husband holland coats and my own riding habit of the same material.

I always wore a sunbonnet up country. From a long

straggling grass I made hats, mats, baskets, dolls hats, and other little things which sold well at church bazaars. The padre of our district had been a schoolmaster at my husband's school in Tonbridge, and he often stayed with us. He and my husband would yarn well into the night, but how I did wish he would refrain a little more from the whisky bottle. His wife was a German, and she gave me many useful domestic hints.

My husband shot seagulls and ducks, and I learned to cure their skins, of which I made winter hats and muffs. Rabbit skins I cured later; they also were turned to good account. As I had a maid for the domestic work, I started to stain all the woodwork inside the house, which consisted of ten sizable rooms. I was fondly hoping that my husband would paint the outside, but for that job he got a man from Christchurch, who also put up a veranda and made a proper approach to the front door. Hitherto a packing case had done duty as a doorstep, much to the amusement of our Christchurch friends who came up to see our home. The banks on each side of the new steps I planted with mesembryanthemum (commonly called "pig's face"), which spread very rapidly and took up much of my time to keep it trim and tidy. I planted banksia roses – very special favourites of mine – so that they could climb up the veranda posts. Geraniums from seeds my mother-in-law sent me turned out to be all sorts of beautiful colours instead of the usual red.

My husband asked his father to send out paper to paper the rooms. When it arrived it was packed in a case with a piano, much to my joy. It was a costly gift though, for we had to have it tuned at once. The tuner came from Christchurch, stayed with us a week, and charged £2. Unfortunately the climate did not suit that piano. Again the tuner came from Christchurch, and treated us to his, not particularly cared for, company for two weeks, apparently enjoying the country life. This piano still refused to keep in tune. Dr. von Haast paid us a visit about this time and sent to Christchurch for a tuning-key, and taught me to tune the old tin-kettle myself. I had so longed for a really good piano, but bad as this one was it gave a good deal of pleasure. But I often think that my practising, and children who stayed with us playing on it, must have got on my husband's nerves.

My husband applied to the Government for assistance to convert the bridle track into a road. The Government, anxious to get the country opened up, willingly assented, and sent up a surveyor, who said we had made far too modest an application, and a much better road could have been surveyed than the old bridle track. But, nevertheless, they went on with widening the bridle track. The work was let out by contract, but we had to supply the timber for a bridge over a creek from our bush quite three miles distant from the site. The men made a saw-pit on a small flat in the bed of the creek that ran through the bush. Our working bullocks had to drag all the timber to the site of the bridge. It was slow work, and the men complained. To expedite matters, and being alone with nothing to do, I took a mare, which was given to bucking and never seemed to have enough work, to the bush so that she could drag the planks up to the top of a long hill for the bullocks to take on to the site of the bridge.

"Betsy Douglas" was a bit light-hearted, and I had to hold her by a rope while I fastened the timber chains on to the boards. After a few journeys, thinking that the mare had had enough and would not run away, I rashly let go the rope to unhitch the timber chains. Off she bolted! I followed her tracks, and at last saw the boards she had been dragging hanging half over a terrible precipice. My heart was in my mouth. I could not even look over the precipice, thinking "Betsy Douglas" must have fallen; but to my great relief, on looking about me, I saw her grazing with some other horses close by. I caught her, patched up the timber chains to the best of my ability, and hitched her on again. She jibbed a bit, and I had difficulty in getting her to the bridge. It must have offended her dignity to do bullocks' work. I quite expected (and hoped) that my husband would remark on the number of planks that were lying on the top of the hill! But never a word did he say. When he wanted his timber chains again, he said, "Whoever has been tinkering with my timber chains?"

"Betsy Douglas" was the only horse I ever saw buck. My husband was riding one day just in front of me when she began to buck. Every buck brought the space between my husband and the saddle greater, another buck and I am sure he and the saddle would have been deposited in the road, but he avoided that by jumping off, and we exchanged horses, he mounting my horse, "Major" and I

"Betsy Douglas", who appreciated my lighter weight, so bucked no more. But I did not appreciate her. She was not equal in comfort to my dear "Major" which was a perfectly trained horse. Australian and New Zealand buckers are credited with releasing themselves from rider, saddle, and bridle. That performance I have never seen though.

There were no stables for horses in those days. The first winter we were in New Zealand we had our riding horses brought home in the evening to have a feed of oats and their cloths put on, but we found it was quite unnecessary. They throve well and kept in good condition on the tussock grass. Colonial horses are very sagacious; perhaps it is owing to their not being stabled. Benighted on the plains, no roads, large holes owing to the rooting of the wild pig, sheep tracks in all directions, leave it to your horse, and he will take you straight home. This was my frequent experience on dark nights, often many miles from home; once where I know my horse had never been before.

A girl friend and I were saved from being enveloped in a quicksand by our horses. We had been picnicking about twenty miles from home. The sun had sunk behind the hill and we had no watches. To avoid being benighted, we decided to take a short-cut by skirting a very dangerous quicksand, which we had been told was quite possible at low tide. Nothing would persuade our horses to go that route, and we gave in to them, thinking they knew best. We heard afterwards that had we insisted on going that way, we should have vanished and never been heard of again.

On another occasion the speed of our horses rescued us from a bush fire. A high wind sprang up suddenly, and the flames got so near that we only reached a river just in time to save ourselves.

Once we had a small bush fire close to our house. My husband lighted the fire a long way off from the house with the wind blowing in the right direction. The wind suddenly changed and got up very high, bringing the flames like a flash of lightning right up to where the weekly wash had been laid out on the tussocks to dry. My maid and I rushed to the rescue, first to save the wash and then to beat out the flames. Of course, the clothes had got smothered with smuts and all had to go into the tub again. My husband and the men followed up the fire, beating with all their might and main, and our united efforts got the fire under control in time to save the house. When the fire was extinguished and all safe, I sank exhausted to the ground, but found that I was getting hotter and hotter. I was sitting on a smouldering tussock. My skirt was of black silk, and that only smouldered away instead of bursting into flames. The result was a bit ludicrous, but would have been serious had the present style of dress been in vogue.

I was glad to see that my husband was at last settling down to work in real earnest. With the help of a man he made an asparagus bed. Neighbours supplied him with plants from their own "bed," and as they were two years old we soon had an abundance of good asparagus. He also made a sea-kale bed. Mushrooms were plentiful, so we enjoyed a good supply of vegetables. The same kind neighbours also supplied us with fruit and other vegetables until our own came to maturity.

One great annoyance to me were the "swaggers." They had another name, but I forget it. Swaggers would arrive at your house and demand a night's lodging. They had with them their blankets and, I suppose, a few other necessaries. They spent their time between sheep shearing and harvest (for which they received very big cheques) "blowing" their money at the accommodation house, where it was the custom to lodge their money with the inn-keeper and drink and eat till it was all spent. They would then hump their swag once more and go from station to station, sometimes professing to want work, but having no intention of doing any until the pinch of poverty really began to make itself felt. The custom of the country was for swaggers to be lodged and fed by "squatters" only, not by "settlers" or "cockatoos".

Squatters were the rich "run" holders who had arrived early in New Zealand and picked out all the best land at pepper-corn rent. They had pre-emptive rights over certain acreages for their improvements, such as shepherds' huts, fencing, etc. Of course, they chose the best land over which to exercise their privileges. In most cases "runs" were heavily mortgaged and the owners were not in a position to exercise their privileges, so some of the best land got into the hands of settlers.

Cockatoos were men of small means who became possessed of very small plots and were somewhat of a nuisance to the more flourishing settlers. We were settlers on a biggish scale. Swaggers used to pretend that they took our place for a "run." Some afternoons I used to see them winding round our mountain road and hiding up till the evening before they came to the house. I turned them when possible, telling them our place was not a "run," and that there was time before nightfall to get to an accommodation house over the hills; but they did not always take the hint.

We had a bad earthquake one evening when there were no less than seven "swaggers" having their supper in the kitchen. The rocking of the house prevented them getting outside. They escaped as soon as they could, and my German maid threw their caps after them, and they were obliged to retire to the whare. If they had brought no provisions with them they must have gone supperless to bed, as they were afraid to return to the house, as it was built of stone. That earthquake split our walls and the veranda posts. The blocks of limestone of which the house was built were very thick – thick enough, in fact, for cupboards in the walls to be built back to back, so fortunately they did not fall.

High north-west winds were very prevalent in the spring where we lived, and were a great drawback. As a warning of their advent small black clouds would appear over the hills which meant three days of a hot high wind. Usually on the third day the wind abated, and then the rain came, which we called "southerly busters." Our house was very exposed to the wind. It had a slate roof, and my husband had lead hipping put down the ridge; but the north-wester would tear up this hipping on the windy side of the house and it would stand up like a frill. The rain followed before there was time to repair the damage, and it is easy to imagine the consequences!

Another earthquake incident occurred when the men who were making the road were camped in the bush. They found a hive of bees in a tree, and sent to ask me if I would rather have the honey or the bees. I decided to have the bees, but before they could take them the cliff, tree, and bees had all slithered into the creek. Dr. von Haast said we had many more earthquakes than we were aware of, and he often felt them when he was geologising in surrounding mountains.

I intended to send to England for my clothes when my outfit wanted replenishing and when we could afford it. But that time never came, and I gave up all idea of going to balls and such-like gaieties in Christchurch. My ball dresses had become old-fashioned, and people in Christchurch dressed very smartly and up to date. The ladies were fond of very smart toilets. They seemed to me to be smarter and to pay more attention to dress than ladies in England. My trousseau was far too plain to suit the taste of Mrs. Cracroft Wilson and her daughter-in-law. The few bonnets that came out with every mail were first critically inspected by Mrs. Cracroft Wilson and her daughter-in-law, who were considered the leaders of fashion in Christchurch. My mother-in-law was very kind in sending me things to replenish my wardrobe, also material from which I made my own dresses. Mrs. Cracroft Wilson had given me plenty of suggestions on the subject of dress, but I decided not to go in for smart things till I really could afford them.

I liked the life in New Zealand, but unfortunately it had to come to rather an abrupt end. The climate, although so bright and sunny, was somewhat treacherous. Very hot days were followed by cold nights. There was little or no twilight. Directly the sun vanished behind the hills, it turned suddenly cold. Clothed in a holland habit, I used to ride the seventeen miles to the post office once a week for letters and papers, and instead of coming straight home invariably went to see friends and was often benighted. Also gardening till it was cold probably caused the chills and severe colds which developed into lung trouble, for after a three-months' illness in Christchurch, the doctors said I would not live if I returned to the rough life up country, and ordered me straight back to England and forbade me even to go up country again.

That order I could not obey, but got home in time to assist in the first shearing. My part consisted in sitting on the stockyard fence and keeping the tally. The lovely mountain air, and riding my pet horse again over the country to pay farewell visits to friends, did me more good than returning to England alone and leaving my husband to follow when all business was settled up, which would have been the case had I obeyed the doctors.

There was no difficulty in letting the place on a short lease to three young men. They did not strike me as being very capable; their hands were too white, for instance! But they promised to look after "Possum," our pet cat, and give him cream and his high chair at table. "Possum" was a prime favourite and the most intelligent cat I have ever known. He bossed all the dogs, and accompanied them with us in our walks. If we got a new dog, he would establish his mastery by boxing his ears, and then he would play with him. Sometimes he would not come in at night when called. He was probably out ratting. In the morning he brought his half-eaten prey and laid it on the window-sill of our bedroom. The grey rat had driven the black native rat away, or nearly so, for it was getting very scarce by the time we left New Zealand.

When we left on horseback, "Possum" rode on my lap till our old house was out of sight, then one of our tenants took him. We heard that "Possum" soon vanished – he did not approve of a kitten the tenants introduced. He had only associated with dogs and humans.

The clip of the wool brought in sufficient cash to pay our passage back to England, which had to be in an old sailing-ship, the *Charlotte Gladstone*, as there were no steamers running either from New Zealand or Australia. The steamer, I think the *London*, that had been running to and from Australia was worn out. The passage in the *Charlotte Gladstone* round Cape Horn took 104 days. After rounding the Horn, we were in a terrific storm for two hours and really in great peril. One huge wave broke in the poop and the captain's cabin, sweeping the saloon and all the cabins.

The *Charlotte Gladstone* was a very old ship and on her last voyage. We had to furnish our own cabins. The passengers' cabins were ranged each side of the saloon. When the big wave broke into the poop and swept into the saloon and the passengers' cabins, we had all retired for the night, but scrambled into dressing-gowns on hearing the screams of the captain's wife. I no sooner opened our cabin door, than I was, by the lurching of the ship, swept off my legs across the saloon and down a passage. My rapid career was stopped by a door, which I cracked by the force with which I was thrown against it. The passengers, then all in the saloon, were aghast, and thought I must be killed. I suppose the water which washed me along saved me. While we passengers were all hurrying to put our belongings on to the saloon table, the ship's carpenter, with help, was able to fill in the breach with mattresses and anything he could lay hold of before a similar wave came. The cold was dreadful. When the storm lulled, the captain served rum all round and complimented the passengers on their behaviour. There were not many passengers on board. My chief friends were the late Head of Christchurch College, going home for his health with his wife and three children and his sister-in-law.

We gave tea-parties on board, to which the captain came. Of course we invited his wife, but she never accepted; nevertheless she got jealous and tried to prevent the steward from saving some milk for our "party"; but at that game she was unsuccessful. Among the passengers there was a young and interesting widow with her tiny baby. Her husband had only recently died.

One day she came up to Mrs H on deck and begged her to come to the captain's wife, as she was lying insensible in her bunk. Mrs. H was puzzled at her appearance and sent for me. I could not diagnose her complaint either, so we sent for the steward. There was no doctor on board – the steward did all the physicking! He stooped down and smelt her breath and said, "She is only drunk." He then shouted into her ear, "Will you have some brandy?" and for answer received a grunt of approval. The captain soon came and took her off to his own cabin, saying he would never take her on a voyage again. Poor man, we were all very sorry for him.

The morning after the storm the sight of the wreckage on deck was an appalling one. A companion ladder had been carried away with two sailors on it by one wave and washed back on to the deck by another wave; the two sailors were also washed back. A great many of the animals we had on board to supply us with fresh meat and the poultry were drowned, so we were threatened with a shortage before we could get home; but with careful management we were able to have enough. We really had a most wonderful escape from being totally wrecked. The rest of the voyage was uneventful. We were becalmed in the tropics; every breath of air seemed to do me good and heal my lung, and by the time we got home no one would believe how ill I had been.

There are a few more reminiscences I would like to add before closing this chapter on my first visit to New Zealand. My brother Pem was living a few miles distant from the town of Auckland, and my husband and I went to visit him there. He had been married for some years and had three children. He married very young, and I, knowing how few nice unmarried girls there were out there in those early days, was anxiously awaiting the introduction to my sister-in-law, but directly I saw her I realised he was lucky in having secured a well-connected, strong, and healthy helpmate. As a boy (and he was little more than a boy when he left England to settle in New Zealand) he was given to falling in love with every girl he met, and used to make me his confidante. I never could understand how he could be off with the old love and on with the new so often and so suddenly. He had evidently not got over his calf love when he first arrived in New Zealand. There were no girls in the sailing-ship he had gone out in; he fell in love on landing with the first girl he met, wrote to me of her charms, and, brother-like, said she was like me! Fortunately she was not responsive to my brother's attentions, and when I made her acquaintance I congratulated myself that she was not my sister-in-law.

At the time of our visit, Pem's wife was not riding so she lent me her saddle. Pem had two horses, and my husband bought a horse for himself, a good weight carrier, for £7. We had delightful rides together. Those rides and occasional drives into Auckland were the chief events of our visit, excepting a whole-day trip to the Thames goldfields. We had put off that trip many times owing to the wet weather. The last day of our visit had come, and as we were determined to see the gold-fields, we set out.

Studio portrait of the author's favourite brother, Walter Pemberton Fooks ("Pem") who emigrated to New Zealand in 1863.

We had to drive to Auckland and then take the wretched little steamer that plied between Auckland and the goldfields. Lack of all comforts did not signify in the day-time, as we could keep on deck and the river Thames was quite smooth. When we arrived at the diggings, Pem's brother-in-law met us in order to show us round. We had permits to go over the Long Drive Mine from a friend who was one of the lucky ones.

On our way back to Auckland we stopped at Wellington for a few hours and saw a friend of mine, an M.P. who was in Wellington at the time, as Parliament was then sitting. He told us the rate at which he was coining money (the amount of which I have forgotten). Within a very short time of this visit doctors ordered him to sell out, as the worry and excitement were turning his brain. He sold out just in time, as the mine was about played out.

We were taken over the Long Drive Mine, shown everything; the whole working from beginning to end was explained to us. Nowadays those methods of working would probably be considered very crude, and it is a pity I cannot remember it all to describe it.

Pem and his brothers-in-law were among the first to secure a section when the goldfield was proclaimed. Their section happened to be next to the Long Drive, but not a scrap of paying quartz had been struck.

Our day was not really enjoyable, as we had so much walking to do, and the mud was thick everywhere. The only way to avoid the mud was to walk on the rails laid for the light railway to convey the quartz to the crushing mills. We made our return journey by night. Of course, there was no accommodation for ladies in the little steamer. The men rolled themselves up in rugs and remained in the saloon. My husband would not allow me to do likewise, as the men were mostly rough diggers. A small compartment, no bigger than a cupboard was assigned to me. There was no furniture, except a common straight-backed chair, so I tried to sleep on the floor! I don't think I had a rug, and I was very wet and cold, as it had been raining the greater part of the day. It was an unusually cold winter for Auckland. In Auckland we had to get the horse and trap, and arrived home very late and very cold, and although we had hot grog, it did not prevent us catching bad colds.

After leaving my brother's house we returned to Canterbury. Just outside Auckland harbour we were nearly wrecked on the Manukau Bar, a dangerous bar and the site of many wrecks. One wave caused us to scrape the bar, but fortunately the following wave carried us over into the open sea, which was frightfully rough. My husband was sea-sick for the first time. He was taken ill so suddenly that he rushed by mistake into a ladies' cabin, and from that time he had more feeling for me. He said he had no idea that sea-sickness was so dreadful. I always was and always shall be a bad sailor.

The Government offered a reward as an incentive to gold prospectors. Some prospectors found their way up to our home and dug a hole in a flat part, but there was no sign of gold. They also "washed the creek," where they found some small garnets supposed to indicate the presence of gold. Dr. von Haast used to say one might as well try to shear wool off "Possum's" back as look for gold in our neighbourhood. A report got about that gold was struck somewhere higher up the Wiapara. A Prospector on his way up stayed with us, and promised to let us know as he passed on his return to Christchurch if he had been successful, so that we might have an early chance of reaping some benefit.

We did not see this prospector again for a long time. He thought he had discovered gold and, wishing to keep his find a secret, returned to Christchurch through quite unknown country. The Government sent an expert back with him, who reported that what the prospector had taken for gold was only mica. Had it been gold, we should not have been told anything about it. As it was, that man had the cheek to come back our way and put up with us. Doubtless there is coal under the limestone, as we found plenty of lignite, but it was not of much use for burning.

Some rivers were bridged even before our arrival in New Zealand, but these bridges were liable to be washed away in high floods.

The first time we rode up to our house the bed of the Ashley River was nearly dry, and I wondered why there was a bridge over it. I did not make use of the bridge, preferring to ride through the shallow river, not realising that the boulders and shingle extending for about a mile constituted the river bed.

The next time we crossed that same river we had a narrow escape from drowning. We were cautioned by friends with whom we had passed the night not to attempt to cross. They begged us to stay with them till the news came that the river had gone down. Disregarding their caution and kind invitation, we went on our way because it was absolutely essential that we should get to Christchurch, as I was expecting my confinement and was going to a nursing-home. On arriving at the banks of the Ashley, we found that there were some heavy drays waiting for the waters to subside. We could also just distinguish some drays on the other side. That bed of shingle and boulders was covered by a torrent of raging water. The bridge that I had thought unnecessary had, all but a small remnant, been swept away. We were in a light trap called a "Yankee wagon," and our getting across alive I must attribute to my husband's presence of mind. He was a strong swimmer and not afraid of water, and he managed the horses well. Of course, our luggage got drenched, and we were fairly wet through, but we escaped safe and sound.

Sometimes the river would rise and become dangerous in a very short space of time. On one occasion we had gone to lunch with a neighbouring "run" holder, and as we were leaving we were informed by one of his men who had just returned from the township with letters that the Wiapara, the river we had to cross, was in flood "up to the saddle flaps, and rising fast." Our host begged us not to start, but we decided to try if we could cross. As the river was some distance from the house, it had had time to rise still higher before we got to the banks. My husband tried to cross at the proper crossing, where there was a sort of road, but found it impossible. We went higher up and tried again. He wanted to cross first and then come back and fetch me. Owing to the noise of the water, which was deafening, he did not hear that I was following on his heels. How the horses managed to avoid the boulders and holes is beyond my comprehension. I stretched my legs along the horse's neck and gave him his head, and he followed close behind my husband's horse, and so we reached the opposite side safely. My husband was rather cross with me for following him, but as I had succeeded so well, we kept to that method in future on similar occasions.

In these early days, when the bridges were washed away, or before they had even been built, the rivers took a terrible toll, especially the Rakaia.[4] In that river Mr. Cracroft Wilson's youngest son was drowned with several stockmen going up to his father's cattle ranch. The bodies were never found. Evidently young Cracroft Wilson was attempting something beyond his powers, for he was a very strong swimmer. Before he left England, where he was educated, he and I were staying with a great-uncle, one of whose young sons was at home on leave from India. They were both quite boys. I and one of my girl cousins used to join them in their walks. One favourite walk was

---

4. The word " Rakaia " means river of death.

in the direction of a distant church. We could just see the steeple, and made for it in as straight a line as we could go. Ditches and thick hedges we managed, but a canal we came to stopped our progress. Young Cracroft Wilson would jump into the canal fully clothed and swim backwards and forwards. He must have been a very strong swimmer, but that is of no avail in a flooded river.

We did not see many Maoris near our house; there was a "Pah" not far away, but I could never persuade my husband to visit it. That same "Pah" was originally on the sea-shore, but the inhabitants moved inland owing to the frequent visitations of the Maoris across the straits from the North Island. The invading Maoris would cross the straits to replenish their larders in the days when there were no wild pigs and when "long pork," as human flesh was called, was their chief meat diet. Suspiciously shaped holes are still found near the shore, and are thought to be the ovens used after the raids.

The Maoris were never so numerous in the South as in the North Island. Their population was kept under by the fondness of the Northerners for "long pork." I very rarely came across a Maori when riding. Occasionally I saw a Maori woman dressed in a riding habit squatting by the roadside smoking a short pipe. Sometimes I would be overtaken by a Maori when riding to the township for letters. He would invariably incite me to a race, and I always kept ahead till we got to a river-bed just outside the township. The river-bed generally consisted of shingle, and if there were any streams they were only very shallow.

I always pulled up at this point. I was not going to gallop my horse over the stones. The Maori would race on, and on my arrival at the township I would find the Maori, in a great state of excitement, telling all and sundry how he had won the race. On one occasion two girls were riding with me when a Maori overtook us. We started to race, and the thrill was too great to pull up at the river-bed, and we tore on, well ahead of the Maori. Unfortunately, the horse of one of the girls fell. He apparently had caught a hind foot in a fore foot; the shoe of the fore foot was wrenched off, and the horse seemed to go head over heels. When we came to the rider's assistance, her head was hanging on the ground; her long habit having caught somewhere, she could not free herself. Her sister was able to get to the horse's head before he had time to start off; but the poor brute was very lame, and that delayed us on our return home considerably.

Returning home one evening, I saw a number of horsemen approaching. I could not imagine what they could be doing so near our home. They proved to be Maoris returning from pig and weka hunting. They had been in the habit of hunting in the mountains near our home, but turned back upon seeing the house. They seemed very pleased when I greeted them with the few words of the language that I knew.

The trouble with the Maoris originally was over land. Why they did not in the early days drive the Pakeha (white man) into the sea was only because of their tribal warfare, of which we made considerable use.

A subsequent visit to New Zealand when I went round the world with my bicycle brought me in contact with the Maoris, and I realised what a lovable and noble people they are; but, of course, years before that time the land question had been settled. Some of the best land was returned to them and Maori reserves allotted, the rentals of which have made them quite a rich people. They are now content and happy.

The cause of the dreadful massacres that were taking place in the North Island during our five year stay in New Zealand and afterwards was in a great measure owing to the Maori making a sort of God of revenge (utu). Every wrong, whether real or imaginary, had to he avenged by the shedding of blood. On his release, a Maori, if he thought he had been wrongfully imprisoned, would avenge himself by the massacre of a number of Pakehas according to the term of his imprisonment, and he did not respect women and children on these occasions.

I shall have more to relate concerning the Maoris when I come to tell of my later trips to New Zealand.

CHAPTER IV

MARRIED LIFE AND ARCHERY

WHEN we returned from New Zealand we lived for nine years with my husband's father in East Kent. My mother-in-law died soon after we came home. I missed her very much. She was always very kind to me and mindful that I was her eldest son's wife. After her death the two unmarried daughters managed the establishment. The life to me was such a contrast to that which we had passed in New Zealand: there too much work, now nothing to do! There was very little society, and that not so intellectual as I had found it in New Zealand.

As my husband had had considerable capital from his father, he did not provide him with riding horses. He was the only one in the family who rode, but having had so much compulsory riding in New Zealand, he did not seem to miss it. We had a few rides together on hired horses, but he soon only hired a good hunter for me, and I had occasional runs with fox- and stag-hounds. He also secured me a room in a friend's house, which became my "den," and I bought an American harmonium. I also got up reading parties. I read German with two girls, whose German governess had just left them, and we took country walks together to study wild flowers. With another girl I read French. An elderly lady who did not know either French or German asked to read English with me, and we started with Shakespeare.

A musical society was formed. I joined and took my place among the Alti. At that time Alti happened to be very scarce. I suppose that is how I came to sing at the Musical Choral Festival at Canterbury Cathedral. I was asked by a musical friend who belonged to the Crystal Palace choir to sing among the Alti at the Handel Festival which was shortly due. She assured me that my voice would not be tested till the festival was over. Much as I would have liked to take part in the festival, want of means prevented me, as it would have entailed not only going up for the festival, but also for rehearsals, so I had to decline.

I joined an Archery Club, and was sent as delegate to the Crystal Palace to shoot when the Grand National Toxophilite Society held their annual meeting. I was lucky on two occasions to win a gold prize. Members of the Grand National Toxophilite Society hardly ever dropped an arrow. I was only a sprat amongst herrings.

Working for bazaars in the autumn and accompanying my husband out shooting, kept me fairly well occupied.

My husband wanted me to shoot and had his boyhood gun made into a breech loader for me, but I never made use of it. I liked walking with the guns, and had as my special companion a bully fox terrier. His tail had never been docked, on account of a report when he was a puppy that docked dogs would in future be ineligible for prizes.

Occasionally, when my husband and I went out shooting alone, he allowed me to take "Zulu" on the leash. When the setter stood still and stiff with extended tail, "Zulu" did the same. When the wounded bird fell to my husband's gun, the retriever's turn came, and I released "Zulu." The race between the dogs was very exciting. If "Zulu" won, the bird was not delivered to hand in quite the condition my husband liked, but he was so very fond of "Zulu" that he did not chastise him. The retriever was never content if he had a blank day. On one such occasion we were eating our luncheon, sitting on a bank close to a farmyard separated from us by a five barred gate. The game bag was empty. The retriever came bounding over the gate with a squealing sucking-pig in his mouth. Of course he had not injured it. On another occasion on a blank morning we were sitting with a friend who had come to shoot with my husband, in a wagonette, in a barn eating our luncheon. The retriever brought us a fowl which seemed to be dead, so we hid it under the seat and decided to hold a consultation as to what should be done with it after luncheon. But the consultation did not come off, for the chicken revived and flew away before our luncheon was finished.

Once every year, either in the spring or summer, my husband and I went away for a month's change. Once we made our chief stay in Guernsey. There I met a friend who took me to the Archery Club, where I had a very enjoyable time. Table turning was all the rage then. We got very curious messages through. We went several times to the little Island of Herm, which was for sale. I had just come in for a few hundred pounds and wanted my husband to buy that island. There was a good landing stage, a shell beach, and a few cottages. Half the island was given up to rabbits, and on part of the shore the burning of wrack or seaweed for manure took place. I would gladly have lived there for a time, to have had my own home again, but my husband preferred to live with his father.

I heard later that the Island of Herm was sold by auction in London for a very small sum. Living as we did with my father-in-law at no expense enabled me to help with the education of the children of my brother Pem, whose widow came to England when he died. The children made a great interest in my rather dull life. To earn money I tried my hand at writing stories, but they only resulted in a waste of paper and ink, so my feeble efforts did not help to swell the contents of my purse.

Nine years passed away, my husband died, and I soon left his father's house. For a whole year I paid visits amongst my relations and friends, who were all very kind to me. Then I went with my brother to Antwerp to see the Exhibition. My brother was an indefatigable sightseer. I, not having sufficiently recovered from the long spell of nursing my husband, suffered too much from fatigue to really enjoy it, but it led me to discover that one could live comfortably on the Continent on a far smaller income than one could in England, especially if able to speak the language of the country.

I took one of my nieces to Leipzig to have the benefit of music lessons and perfect her German. My old German governess was then residing there, and I left my niece in her charge and accepted an offer to chaperone two girls to Italy, which enabled me to give my niece more advantages than I otherwise could have done. On returning to Leipzig in the spring, I took my niece home via Brussels and Antwerp, stopping en-route at interesting places, intending to, and thinking to, give her pleasure and a certain amount of education, but she was homesick, which at the time I did not notice, neither did I realise that she did not, like me, suffer from "Wanderlust," a complaint which years have not lessened, for at eighty-eight I am as keen on travelling as ever. From that time I was very seldom in England. I have travelled all over the Continent several times, before, after and during the years I was cycling. My last visit to Spain was shortly before the Revolution. I joined a touring party, and we visited many places of interest. Wherever we went we noticed marked discontent with the then Government, and it was apparent that Spain was on the eve of a revolution; in fact, we only arrived home a few days before the Revolution took place. I was secretly sorry not to have been in the country at the time.

Of course, during the Great War I could not go on the Continent, but my" Wanderlust" carried me on my bicycle many hundreds of miles in the United Kingdom.

After my husband's death I sometimes happened to be staying at Bowman's Lodge with my father on the occasion of "Grand Nights" at the Middle Temple, of which my brother Willie was a member, and of Gray's Inn, of which my father was then a member and Bencher, he having left the Middle Temple when he "took silk." On "Grand Nights" at Gray's Inn ladies were entertained in the gallery. On the last occasion that I was in the gallery, the Benchers entertained King Edward VII, then Prince of Wales.

The Prince arrived very late. The "Loving-cup" was handed round before he sat down. His late arrival caused him to stay over the scheduled time, and, looking from the gallery and seeing no sign of an adjournment, I began to fear my father would miss the last train home; he was then an old man and slow in his movements. All I could do was to summon his clerk and tell him my difficulty and ask him to find someone who could procure permission from the Prince for my father to retire. This he managed, and it caused the Prince to realise that he had overstayed his time, and he immediately left the table. In the meantime to hurry up my father, I found myself in the gentlemen's cloakroom face to face with the Prince of Wales, who did not overwhelm me with smiles. At any rate, I obtained a good view of him. My bird's-eye view from the gallery gave him the appearance of a magnified peg-top, for his figure was rotund; but a closer view banished that impression, for he was really of a commanding appearance and had expressive eyes.

On another occasion I attended a ball at the Middle Temple to chaperone one of my nieces, who, to my horror, I beheld dancing with a coloured man who wore a large turban.

CHAPTER V

NEW ZEALAND AGAIN

MY second visit to New Zealand was in 1883, about two years after the death of my husband. I went on business. The three young men to whom we had let our old home left when their lease was up. To the next tenants my husband granted an option to purchase at the end of their lease. I had always hoped that we should return to New Zealand at the expiration of our first tenants, lease. I tried to persuade my husband, but in vain, not to grant a purchasing clause in the new lease. I felt all along that the advice to do so that he was receiving from the lawyer in New Zealand was more to the interest of the new tenants than to ours. Owing to the death of Sir Cracroft Wilson and through other circumstances, our small affairs had drifted into this same lawyer's hands. I never believed in or trusted him.

Unfortunately, Sir Cracroft Wilson did, and made him one of the executors and trustees of his immense estate. Fraudulent use was made of that and many other trusts, and my small one among them. Eventually he was found out and brought to book. The case will be remembered by many, it was so notorious. The real culprit, the lawyer, was in England when the crash came, and his younger brother in New Zealand, a partner in the firm, was crossed off the Rolls. The managing clerk was sent to penal servitude. I do not know what became of him, but the real culprit escaped scot-free. His younger brother was eventually reinstated.

Exploring for coal enticed him to use trust funds, and I heard later, I don't know with what truth, that coal was found by others in the districts he had been exploring. It was very unfortunate that the punishment fell upon the wrong heads.

It was to receive personally the money due for the purchase of our property that I went out to New Zealand this time. I had previously written to the tenant instructing him that I would be in New Zealand to receive in person from him the purchase price of the property. He disregarded this instruction of mine. We were defrauded in more ways than one. Christchurch Cathedral had been built of limestone from our property, but we never received a penny for it.

I went out by an Orient steamer. Christmas Day was spent in the Red Sea. It was too cold and rough for the children travelling third class to have the Christmas tree prepared for them. Money for the tree had been collected on board, and I had been deputed to lay it out at Port Said. Everything there was expensive with the exception of cigarettes, and I was able to get very little fit for children.

I landed at Suez and walked with a fellow passenger to Old Suez, then little more than ruins. In walking down the main street it suddenly occurred to me that I had read somewhere that it is advisable in Eastern towns not to walk close to the houses, but to keep to the middle of the street. I had no sooner turned that brilliant remembrance to account than splash came the contents of a utensil on my companion's head, covering him with its evil-smelling contents, of which grease seemed to be the chief ingredient. I gave that young man a wide berth when returning along the sand to our ship.

We stopped to coal at a small coral island, one of a group near the Seychelles in the Indian Ocean. Excepting this island, which was only a coaling station, the group of islands belonged to France. Nothing seemed to grow on them but coconuts, and the only industry was copra making. The only white resident on the English island was a retired Orient captain. His life was very lonely, and as he could not speak French he was unable to associate with the inhabitants of the other islands. One can well imagine how he looked forward to the arrival of the Orient boats when they stopped to coal. I spent the greater part of my time while on the island collecting shells. On leaving, I gave the lonely captain all the books I could spare.

To my horror, when I started sorting the shells in my cabin, many of them began to walk about! The shells were mostly the abodes of the hermit crab. These crabs and their shells I kept till we reached the Semaphore, the port for Adelaide. I turned them out there, and wondered whether they would survive and become a puzzle in the future to some naturalist. Before reaching Adelaide we had put in at Albany, the most important point of Western Australia. In those days natives used to come down to the newly arrived boats and display their skill in throwing boomerangs to amuse the passengers. In Adelaide there were also many natives to be seen.

Eventually I arrived at Christchurch, where I had a long and very unpleasant interview with the lawyer. He did his best to pass me and my business on to the managing clerk, saying he knew my affairs even better than he did. Failing that, he tried to persuade me to allow him to invest the money he had received from the tenants of our property, who, disregarding my instructions, had paid it to him. At length I was able to leave the lawyer's office armed with a cheque for the amount due, and started off immediately to visit the widow of Sir Cracroft Wilson, who had kindly been to Lyttelton to meet me, but unfortunately we had missed each other. I stayed with her on a long visit, and found that she too had been suspicious about the lawyer's integrity.

I spent my whole time while in New Zealand visiting relations and friends both in the North and South Islands. The kindness and hospitality I received I very much appreciated. I got plenty of riding, and saw more of station life than I had seen previously, especially when staying at Mount Peel. I can recall the beauties of the Orari Gorge and also a bit of real native bush near my host's house. One day, when penetrating the dense undergrowth of that bush, I lost my bearings, and only regained them on hearing the sound of a loud dinner-bell.

Of course, during the years since my residence in New Zealand great changes had taken place, rivers had been properly bridged, railways constructed, tussock grass was fast disappearing, giving place to good English grasses, which carried many more sheep to the acre. The disappearance of the tussock and the wild ferns accounted for the shortage of the wild pig and the weka.

I stayed with some old friends in the neighbourhood of our late home, and we rode and drove and walked to the old haunts. One walk was to the top of Mount Grey (5,000 ft.) – the mountain stood some miles away at the back of our house. I always had a great wish to get to the summit. One Christmas before my husband and I left New Zealand some children were staying with us, and we started off one day with our "nose-bags," hoping to get as far as a "bush" we could see, through glasses, in one of the gullies of the mountain. We toiled through high tussocks and fern interspersed with a growth called "lawyer," on account of its propensity for not letting you free yourself easily. If you were unfortunate enough to get into its grasp, you generally escaped with loss of fragments of garments. We crossed a swamp by following each other along a wire fence.

Long before we reached the "bush" we were making for, we had consumed the contents of our "nose-bags."

We found good water there to quench our thirst and then had a good run down the mountainside through the "bush." The "bush" was very dense, and the high trees above the "bush" made it so dark that I thought it was getting late. I had no watch. It was midwinter, and there was very little twilight. We had wandered in the "bush" till I had lost my way. On returning to the stream where we had drunk, I found the water running the reverse way to what I had expected; for some little time we had been wandering in quite the wrong direction. I was a bit afraid that the children might get frightened, especially two of them who had come from Christchurch and had never been upcountry before. The two other children were used to country life and had the same taste for exploring and mild adventure as myself. By following the flow of the water we got out of the "bush" and found it was still quite light and we arrived home in good time, rather tired and very hungry.

CHAPTER VI
JUSTICE IN TASMANIA

IN 1887 I accompanied my father to Tasmania. He was then a Q.C., and went out to conduct a case against the Tasmanian Government. He was not a good traveller and had never been for a long sea voyage. He had anticipated this journey for some time, and prepared me by saying that should the legal business in connection with the Railway Company and for which he had always been standing Counsel, necessitate him to conduct a case in Hobart, would I go with him? So I was not surprised to receive a telegram when I was in Paris to say he was starting for Tasmania in a fortnight's time. I hurried back, and on arriving at my father's house found my stepmother occupied packing two large Saratoga trunks for my father to take out with him. With great difficulty I cut down some of the unnecessary clothing. Boots were a special hobby of his, and I discovered that my stepmother was going to pack twenty pairs, but I managed to cut them down to fourteen pairs.

The author's father, William Cracroft Fooks, Q. C., aged 51.

We went as far as Melbourne in a P&O steamer, the *Massilia*, and had a very favourable passage, my father keeping well the greater part of the time. His only indisposition was due to his insisting on sampling all the different wines on the ship, and at Brindisi, where we landed for a few hours, he bought some native wine, which he took back to the ship with him. He was taken ill after sampling the Brindisi wine, which was probably new, and he hoped to rectify matters by taking some whisky; but the doctor had to be called, and he soon recovered under the doctor's ministrations.

At Melbourne we had to tranship to a small steamer to go on to Hobart. My father spent his seventieth birthday on that steamer. Among our fellow passengers from Melbourne were Dr and Mrs Madden and a daughter of theirs. Dr Madden was the leading Counsel in the Railway case for the Tasmanian Government. They were all very pleasant, and we stayed at the same hotel in Hobart. Dr Madden later on was knighted.

The "Case" was to come on the day after our arrival at Hobart. My father had to see the Governor of Tasmania, Sir Robert Hamilton, as soon as we arrived, as he had to be created a Q.C. of Tasmania before he could appear in Court to conduct his case. His two juniors had been appointed in Tasmania.

We had fortunately arrived early in the morning, which gave ample time to get through the preliminaries. I was busily employed unpacking Father's belongings. The fourteen pairs of boots became a problem – the newspaper they were wrapped in was sticking to them. They formed quite a mountain to face my father on his return to the hotel to luncheon. The hotel "boots" declined to clean any but what were required for present wear. Father vowed he would clean them himself!

There was a reception at Government House in the afternoon, which we had to attend, also a dinner party in the evening. Father spent a greater part of the morning with Sir Robert Hamilton. No Q.C. had ever been created in Tasmania. Luckily Father had brought his English Patent with him, which served as a precedent. The dinner at Government House was very pleasant. I was sitting near two of Sir Robert's sons. They had been at St. Paul's School and knew one of my nephews, who was on the foundation of the School at that time. Lady Hamilton invited me to go to the races with her the following day, but I was obliged to decline that and other gaieties, as Father wanted me to be in Court while the case was on and to devote my whole time to him.

The following morning my father got up early and, giving me the slip, went out and bought brushes and all the paraphernalia necessary for cleaning his boots, but, fortunately, there was no time before he had to be in Court, where, also fortunately, he was detained too long to enable him to carry out his intentions before I devised a plot. Seeing that the chambermaid and "boots" were fond of each other's company, I "made love" to the chambermaid, and asked her to get round and manage the "boots," telling her that he would receive a good tip if on Father's return he found all his boots cleaned. Father got back to the hotel for luncheon, and there were the boots in his room all clean and in a row. Of course, he could polish them up to his heart's desire at any time, so that difficulty was got over by a little diplomacy which I discovered had often to be practised during that trip; but it did not always end with such success. Father made use of his riding boots, for we hired horses and rode one afternoon, Dr. Madden's daughter accompanying us.

One day a special train was chartered to take all those who were connected with the case to the centre of the island, to visit a large apple farm. The hotel where the luncheon was provided was very primitive. Apparently never before had its resources been so heavily taxed, although I suspected that some of the provisions had come in the train from Hobart with us. Certainly the champagne had, for there was not a proper champagne glass on the table. I drank mine out of a tooth glass.

The "Case" was not to be mentioned on penalty of a fine of £5. Many witnesses from Australia connected with the railways in North, South, and West Australia were of the party, and most of them were staying at the same hotel as ourselves. We were taken to see the apples being packed which were destined for the English market; that and the luncheon took up all the time of our stay. While in Tasmania we were given free passes for all the different railways in Australia, and we were told we could renew them when the time for renewal became due. I did not renew mine and lived to regret it, for in after years I was often in Australia and could have made good use of free passes.

Another outing, arranged, I believe, by the Government in my father's honour, was a trip up Mount Wellington. A horse was provided for Father, but he preferred to walk, although I feel sure he had never done such a climb before.

My father had a daily refresher of £100 – his retainer was £1,000. The daily refresher he gave into my keeping.

On the afternoon of the day on which judgment was given, Father and I had to separate, he to attend to the winding up of some legal affairs, and I to make farewell calls and to leave his card. When we met later, he told me he had paid his final refresher into a bank, to be ready for him when he returned to Tasmania. He said that he liked the country, and that he had enjoyed himself so much that he intended to come back again. It was too late to get the money out of the bank that night, and we left Hobart early the next morning before the banks were open.

From Hobart we went on to La Trobe in the centre of the island, where we had promised to stay with some connections. We missed the train they expected us by, so telegraphed the time of a later train. It was a wet evening, and a covered conveyance was engaged to meet us at the station. It was a very old, dilapidated covered wagonette with broken springs. We were told that when our host went to hire it to meet us at the station, chickens were roosting in it, but as it was that or nothing, he was obliged to engage it to meet us at the station. My father did not like the jolting over the rough road after our long and tiring railway journey.

Our host had a large family, two sons and several daughters, and they were clever at arranging glorious picnics for our entertainment. One picnic was to a Government reserve, a rough rocky sort of place composed of what looked like shale, where it was expected oil would be found; but no borings had been commenced then. I have often wondered if oil was found later.

As there were so many young people in the party, I was not so tied by attending to and looking after my father. He liked hunting for curios to take home. He asked me if a white opossum skin was worth buying, and if so, how much ought he to pay for it. The following day we went on a kangaroo hunt. Father had found a half-caste huntsman and engaged a large brake to take the whole family, as the hunt was to take place some distance away in open "bush" similar to Australian "bush."

We did not have much sport. The huntsman pointed out the spoor of the kangaroo which he judged to be a large one from the length of the spoor of the tail. That kangaroo we did not find, but sighted a smaller one, which we followed up. I managed to keep up with the huntsman and his sons – all the others were left behind – but we did not catch up with the kangaroo, so gave up the chase. I asked the huntsman what Father ought to give for a white opossum skin. He answered that he knew the skin I referred to and that my father wanted it, but that it belonged to one of his sons, who had just been telling him that he wanted to give it to me because I ran so fast. So I became the proud possessor of that opossum skin, and when I got home I had it properly dressed, and only parted with the remains of it last spring (1931). It had become a hopeless prey of the moths during my frequent absences from home.

Our pleasant stay at La Trobe came to an end and we trained on to Launceston, where we intended to take the boat to Melbourne and hoped to pick up the *Massilia* on her return journey after her month's stay in Australia. We spent a few days at Launceston. We took one drive of sixty miles to go over a gold-mine and another drive of sixty miles with the same buggy and horse to look over a farm that Father had heard was for sale. He had an idea that he would like to buy it. The final three or four miles to the farm was through the "bush," but there was no road. We met a horseman who said he could guide us to the farm, and if the buggy would follow him we would avoid the trees, stumps and rocks. He assured us that one of the sons of the owner was there, and that he would give us something to eat and see us safely through the "bush" again.

It was then nearing early-dinner time and had begun to rain, and the man who was guiding us wanted to get back to his dinner. We accepted his kind offer to guide us and started off, he riding in front and I driving the buggy close behind. Father insisted on getting out to walk, but could not keep pace with the horses, which delayed us considerably. Soon we came to some shallow water, so my father was obliged to get into the buggy again, and I made him realise that our guide wanted to get back to his dinner, so he remained in the buggy and we progressed a bit better, and at last arrived at the paddocks near to the house. The horseman descended to open the gate for us, saying, "You will be sure to find someone at the house who will give you something to eat and see you back through the "bush," " took off his hat and bade us farewell, and returned the way that we had come with a speed that showed that he wanted his dinner.

We knocked, but received no answer; there was nobody in, but we entered and took shelter from a heavy shower of rain. We hunted about, but could not find anything to eat. My father had fortunately wrapped up and pocketed the leg of a duck at breakfast, which he ate. We soon realised that the farm was no good to us, but we had to wait till the weather cleared before starting back. It was getting chilly, and Father would insist on walking again.

When we got outside the paddock he tried without any success to make out our wheel marks, but the rain had obliterated them all. I was glad he did not get into the buggy, for he would have wanted the reins, and I knew by giving the horse his head we would be all right, the Australian horses being so clever at finding their way. Occasionally I saw a wheel mark in a sheltered spot and called out to Father that we were all right, but would not check the horse by waiting for him for fear he should want to drive and not leave the horse to find his own way. We at length arrived at the piece of shallow water and

Father got into the buggy, and from there I remembered the way. We halted to give the clever animal his nose-bag, which he richly deserved. I felt very grateful to that horse, for to have been "bushed" for the night would have been serious for my father, as he was very wet, and also the steamer that was to take us to Melbourne was due to start the next morning. We were benighted, but the horse knew the way and landed us safely at our hotel.

Tasmania struck me as being a sort of sleepy hollow, a place in which to pass a pleasant old age, if only possessing small means. The climate is very beautiful. On later visits (the last in 1914) Hobart did not appear to me to be much altered; just the same sleepy place and surroundings unaltered, just as they were when Father and I went for those long drives years previously. Much land seemed to have been allowed to go out of cultivation, and rose briers had quite taken possession of the ground.

We spent one night at Melbourne, and took the train the next day to Adelaide. The river Murray was in flood, but the train got through all right. We spent a few pleasant days in Adelaide, and were entertained by Chief Justice Way, who was most anxious for us to stay in the hills with him, where he had his country house, but it meant missing the *Massilia* and spending another month in Australia. The longer stay would have been delightful, but I was anxious to see my father home again.

On the way home we landed and had a few hours at Malta and Gibraltar. Father did not sample all the wines as he did on the outward journey, and abstained entirely in the hot weather. He arrived in Plymouth in good health, in fact looking much better and younger than when he set out.

At Plymouth, where we took train for London, Father said he intended to look after me for the rest of the journey in return for all my care and attention to him. I was having a pleasant chat with a fellow passenger as the train reached Taunton. I did not notice that my father had left the carriage till the train was slowly crawling out of the station, and then I saw him on the platform with a glass of beer in his hand. I would have jumped out, but could not get the carriage door open in time. I got out at Bristol, and after hours spent there watching for every train which came through from Taunton, I took a train back to Taunton, and on alighting, the station master said, "Are you looking for an old gentleman with a white hat? I put him in an excursion train; he must have arrived at Paddington hours ago."

I had time to get some supper, and the station master put me in a night mail train. I arrived at Paddington very early in the morning and had to wait till I could get the registered luggage, for which I fortunately had the tickets. It was Sunday, and there were no official about, so I had a long wait.

On reaching my father's house, I found that he had arrived quite safely, and that he had been sending to the local station to meet every train except the one I did arrive by! Father had arrived on the Saturday night; I did not until Sunday morning. We had sent my brother, who then lived in London, a telegram from Plymouth to say we had landed, and curiously enough he happened to be in the same train as I was and on his way to welcome my father at Bowman's Lodge. I did not know that till we met on the platform at Crayford. " 'Where is Father?" he exclaimed. "I don't know," I replied, "but here is his hat," which was a duplicate he had left in the carriage with all his other impedimenta when he alighted to get the beer at Taunton.

CHAPTER VII

TRAMP SHIP TO ARMENIA, 1896

IN the summer of 1896 I became interested in the Armenians through attending drawing-room meetings held to raise funds to send out a delegate to investigate the alleged cruelty of the Turks to the Armenians. Armenians spoke at the meeting, and they aroused the spirit of adventure, still alive in me, which led me to accept the offer to become the delegate.

I was to get full particulars and information from certain Armenians. The information proved very scanty. I gathered that the expedition was to be conducted as secretly as possible, in order that it should not become known to the Turks, who were doing their utmost to prevent any strangers from entering Armenia. It was decided that I should find my way into the country as a butterfly collector, that I was to land at Trebizond on the Black Sea, and to go to Diarbekir and Van. I was given

The passport photo of the author taken in Brighton, 1896

introductions to some Armenians in London through whom I should find a suitable interpreter to take with me.

Again the information I got was far from helpful, so I set to work to prepare for the journey, using my own discretion. I let my house at Hove, and went up to London to get my outfit, etc.. I first went to the reading-room of the British Museum and studied the Asiatic journals and the features of the country I was to pass through. I found that to get into Armenia proper from Trebizond, fairly high mountain ranges had to be crossed, the passes of which I might find blocked with snow if my departure were delayed for long, and that the only way of getting to my destination would be by employing an army of Kurds to clear the way, which did not look very promising for my butterfly-collecting expedition!

A passport had to be procured, which involved a personal interview with Lord Salisbury. Before he affixed his signature he gave me kindly advice as to how I was to comport myself if in personal touch with the Turks. Then I had to have an interview with Mr. Butler, head of the butterfly department at the Natural History Museum, and he told me something about the butterflies I might find there.

Mr. Butler was an old friend. He used to spend his holidays with his wife's relations at Sittingbourne in Kent, near where my husband and I were then living. Mr. Butler's hobby was birds, and his wife and one or two other ladies accompanied him on his bird-nesting expeditions. I was often invited to join the party, and, being well acquainted with the country and the haunts of the birds, was able to make myself of use. Mr. Butler provided me with poison bottle and net, and told me how best to preserve specimens for him to set up on my return.

I found an interpreter in a medical student who was a protége of the mission then run by the Grattan Guinnesses at Bow, with whom by marriage I was connected. He was a Russian Armenian and entitled to wear the Fez, which I was told would be a protection for him in case of any unpleasantness or difficulties we might encounter if we came in contact with Turks; but he did not come with me, after all.

Through friends I secured a passage in a tramp steamer. She was a trading steamer calling at many ports before her destination in the Black Sea. I bought a side-saddle and sleeping-bag, besides revolver and cartridges and sundry other necessaries. Through my friend the late Mrs. Amery, mother of Mr. L. S. Amery, M.P., I got some really useful information, as her father and other relations had been so much in touch with the Turks during their connection with the Turkish Embassies. One of Mrs. Amery's relations to whom she gave me an introduction was Mrs. Richter, wife of Dr. Richter, well known in connection with Italian pictures at the National Gallery, Trafalgar Square. Mrs. Richter's father had been Ambassador at Brusa, and she had spent much time there and been much in contact with Armenians, so she was able to tell me much about them and their characteristics. My friend Cosmo Monkhouse gave me a lesson on ceramics, and pointed out fragments of tiles and china, specimens of which I was to try to procure for him.

All this time I had been in constant correspondence with an Armenian who caused me so much delay that I began to question whether it was not getting too late in the autumn to get through the mountain passes to Armenia. In the final letter I received the writer expressed an opinion that I was not sufficiently imbued with the cruelty of the Turks towards the Armenians to undertake the mission. I was supposed to be going with an unbiased mind to investigate, and it seemed to me that the best thing I could do was to forward the whole correspondence to the clergyman in Scotland who held the fund that had been collected, and tell him that I thought it was too late to try to get to Armenia that autumn as a butterfly collector. His answer came by return of post: "Take the fund and start directly." As I had not drawn on the fund for my outfit and passage on the tramp steamer, I felt at liberty to act as I thought best, which was to go round the Mediterranean in the tramp, land at every port where she stopped, and pick up all the information I could, not attempting to get into Armenia, as it would be October before the ship got away from London.

I wrote and thanked the clergyman for his offer of funds, which I declined; but I also promised to keep him informed of anything respecting the treatment of the Armenians at the hands of the Turks that I might hear or learn. Early in October I received my summons to be on board the tramp. When I arrived, all was confusion. Rumours were afloat that the steamer was unseaworthy and that all the officers had resigned on that account. A Board of Trade Official was on board, the lifeboat was being repaired, and new officers had arrived. The tramp was very dirty and malodorous owing to some rotten potatoes in the hold. My cabin was absolutely devoid of necessaries. Owing to the alertness of the new Captain and the insistence of the Board of Trade, the needful repairs were effected, and we got off after a few days' delay.

There were two other passengers besides myself – young men going to Syria to start a horse farm. There were four officers and a German steward, who also acted as cook, and a full complement of sailors. There was a bath in the tramp which was filled when required with sea water by a pipe from the deck. It did not seem to be much in request by anyone but myself, and to get it filled was quite a ceremony, commencing with orders from the Captain.

The tramp was of an old-fashioned build with a "well." The German cook-steward prepared plain and quite wholesome food, but onions predominated! The Captain took the head of the table. At our first meal he came without his coat and his shirt-sleeves were turned up. The first officer, who had seen better days, had changed his coat and washed his hands. He had been unfortunate – he had lost his capital cattle ranching in South America. He had been Captain of a yacht, but bad luck had brought him to be first officer on board a tramp. His example of making himself tidy and washing his hands before meals was soon followed by the Captain. I do not think the Captain at first liked having a lady passenger. The two other officers dined later; they were keeping watch on deck while we had our meal.

I don't think anyone on board possessed a book besides the first officer and myself, and as I always travel as light as possible, I had only a small supply; but I soon found plenty of occupation for my needle in keeping the flags in repair – the duty of the fourth officer – and doing mending for the Captain and the other officers. By this means we soon established a good understanding, and in return for my needlework no objection was raised when I wished to go ashore at every port as soon as "pratique" was obtained and all Customs formalities observed. The weather was perfect all the way down the Channel and the Bay of Biscay quite calm.

Malta was the first port we stopped at, and the discharging and reloading took two days. I was put ashore as soon as possible, and wandered about the island, returning at night to sleep on board. At Malta I was mistaken for the Captain's wife and was offered commission on the stores supplied to the boat if I would use my influence with my supposed husband to procure his custom! The melons had not been harvested; they were growing everywhere. I found my way to the bay where Saint Paul landed, and, strange to say, saw there the only snake I encountered in the island, but feel sure, judging from the shape of its head, that it was not a poisonous one. In Valetta the grapes were abundant and very cheap, so I secured a huge basketful to take back to the tramp, and on board we all partook freely of them.

We arrived at Bengazi, our next port of call, during the night. The Captain landed me as early as he could in the morning, and I saw many sights that I should have missed, owing to the heat, if I had landed later. Two women I saw sitting at a mill grinding corn just as described in the Bible. Camels were coming in from the desert laden with esparto grass, which I came across later on my return to England at paper mills being used for making paper.

I took a walk out into the desert to the wells, where camels and other animals were being watered, and returned to the tramp for early dinner. To my surprise I found that the two young men passengers had not landed but I inspired them with a wish to explore by my enthusiastic description of the sights I had seen; so after dinner they went ashore, but failed to see anything that interested them, and seemed disappointed that they had not come across a slave market which their guide had promised to take them to. Of course there was no slave market, but that is the bait generally held out by guides to those who in Australia and New Zealand are called "new chums." We lay off Bengazi for the night and, before starting the next morning, the two other passengers and I did a flourishing trade in empty beer bottles for melons and pomegranates. The melons were the large green sort with black seeds, very watery, and the pomegranates, of course as usual, all pips.

Our next port was Alexandria, where the Captain expected to remain till late the next day. He landed me at the quay. He told me he would be waiting for me there on my return from Cairo, whither I was anxious to go. He gave me that day and the following to remain on shore. I made straight for Cook's office before going to the station to take train for Cairo.

Before leaving England my father's faithful old clerk Sherwood gave me an introduction to a nephew who was a manager of Cook's office at Cairo. I learned, however, that he had not yet arrived for the season. His name was a "power" and probably he is still remembered by Messrs Cook & Co. The passenger I best remember on the train was an English lady who gave me useful advice and hints how to deal with the Arabs, the most important of which was on no account to accept any kind of gift from them. I observed how she civilly declined figs which an Arab in the carriage offered her.

It was quite dark when we reached Cairo, but I was met by one of Cook's agents, who had received a telegram from Alexandria instructing him to meet me. He took me to a hotel, where the charges were moderate. Before retiring for the night, I made arrangements to start quite early for the Pyramids. In those days there were neither trams nor trains available, and my only way to get there was by hiring a small victoria and pair. There were some guests at the hotel who also intended visiting the Pyramids the next day, but their arrangements were already made before I arrived, and also they were not

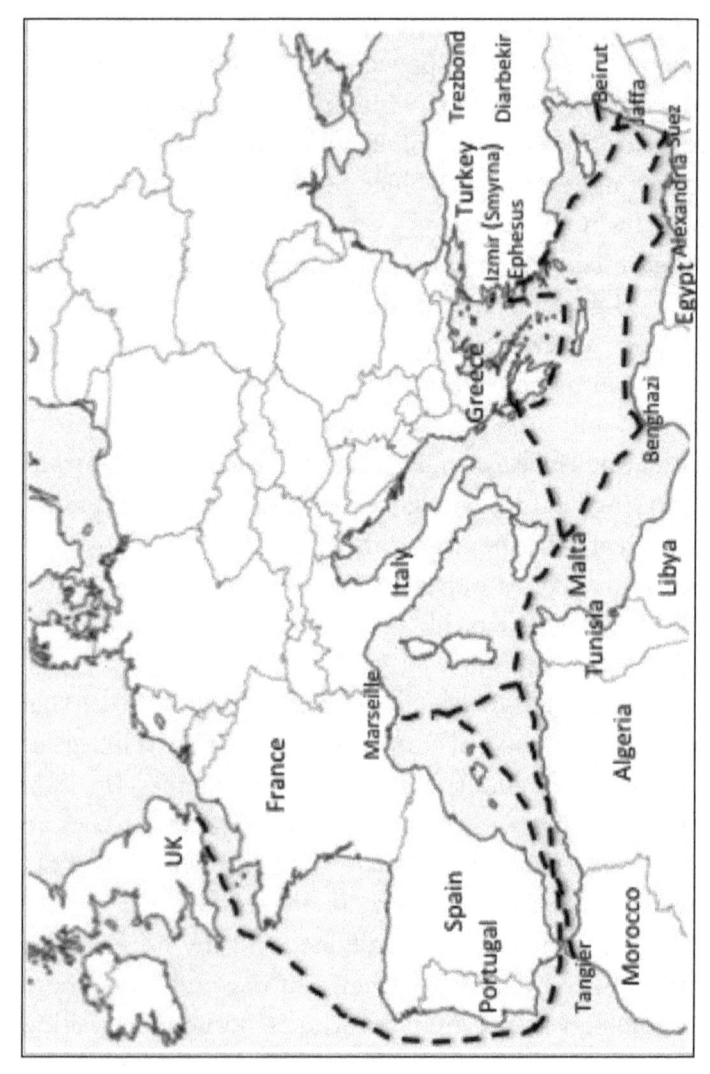

Map 1: The voyage by tramp steamer to Turkey

leaving early enough for me, who had to make the most of the one day I was allowed for seeing what I could of Cairo.

The victoria, drawn by a nice little pair of Arab horses, came to fetch me in good time. The driver was an Egyptian and Mohammedan. To enable me to gain all the information I could, I mounted to the box-seat next to the driver, and very soon took the reins out of his hands.

I was fairly puzzled to distinguish between the different nationalities we met on the road. My driver enlightened me on that and many other subjects. He also told me a little about his own home and domestic arrangements. He said he had not yet his full complement of wives, which was four for a working man. He had only three, but said he intended to go to Paris and get a Frenchwoman for his fourth wife. I asked him to take me to his home when we returned to Cairo. I told him I should like to make the acquaintance of his three wives. That he said was impossible, as his three wives would take me for the fourth one he intended to have! Although I pointed out to him that my age would get him over that difficulty, even that did not gain me admittance to his home. He said he had a favourite among his wives, but did not let the others know it. I gave him a fig to take to his favourite wife, but he said he would give it to a brother, for as regards presents he always gave to all his wives alike.

I asked him how it would be when he brought home his intended French wife. He said that for a time home would be very unpleasant to him, but they would soon settle down and become reconciled, chiefly because a fourth wife would lighten the labours of the other three. We passed several rough carts drawn by oxen with four fat women sitting in the carts with presumably their husbands steering the oxen. The drive was full of interest. Hippopotami, with their snouts just above the water, were in the Nile. I saw hyenas in the distance in the desert. The driver told me to give my purse and its contents into his keeping, as otherwise I should be lightened of it by the Arabs at the Pyramids. Thinking that my purse would be safer in my own keeping, I thanked him and drew his attention off the subject of the purse while I quickly put it into a safe pocket in an under garment.

Shortly before reaching Ghizeh and the Mena Hotel, the driver drew up close to a crowd of Arabs on the lookout for "prey," and told me I must have one of them to protect me while at the Pyramids, and to select one from the group. There was a perfect sea of faces gazing up at me, all in a state of great excitement and expectation. I selected a young man, handsome and honest looking. The driver signalled to him to jump into the victoria, seized the reins out of my hands, lashed up the horses, and we simply seemed to fly with the crowd of Arabs with their flowing white robes in hot pursuit.

We were soon at the foot of the Pyramids at the Mena Hotel. I alighted from the box-seat of the victoria and started with my Arab guide immediately, as I had not much time to spare, up the ascent through thick sand towards the Pyramids. Before long the whole mob of Arabs caught us up. My guide seemed quite helpless amongst them all, and most of my breath and energy, which I needed for walking through the deep sand and up the ascent, was expended in trying to keep the Arabs from touching me. They cuffed and pulled at my clothing, all yelling for "baksheesh." One man with a long stick pretended to keep them from me, but in spite of that our progress was very slow.

On reaching the top of the rise, I managed to see the Sphinx and the entrance to the big Pyramjd, but to attempt to enter the galleries and chambers was out of the question because of the Arabs, so I made my way back to the victoria, still followed and persecuted by the crowd. The Arab with the long stick was particularly pressing for baksheesh, maintaining that I would have been murdered but for his intervention, whereupon I told him I was English and under the protection of the English Government, and if anything happened to me they would be answerable. They had mistaken me for a French lady, so I told them to look at my boots, asking them if they had ever seen a French lady with such thick footwear, and on hearing and seeing that I was of English nationality, their demeanour changed at once, and we walked back to the carriage quite amicably together.

They were very keen to effect a change of money, which would, I explained to them, have been of great advantage to me. They were so insistent that I told them that when I got back to the carriage I would change as much as they liked, implying that I had no money with me. On reaching the carriage and again mounting the box, I quietly produced my purse from my underneath pocket. The expressions on the faces of the same crowd I had seen on my arrival were vastly changed when they discovered that I had had my money with me all the time! After only paying my young guide, the driver whipped up the horses, and we left the Arabs running off to another carriage full of tourists that had just arrived. As it was so early in the morning when I left Cairo for the Pyramids, no other tourists were there, so I had had the full brunt of the annoyance of the Arabs all to myself.

On our way back to Cairo the driver drew my attention to a smart, handsome Arab mounted on a splendid horse. He told me he was the son of the Sheik of the Pyramids, and that he was too heavy a weight for the young horse he was riding. He asked me if I would allow him to drive in the victoria, and said that the servant riding behind would take charge of his master's horse. I gladly assented, being pleased to make the Sheik's acquaintance. He got into the victoria. I felt a bit undignified, being still on the box-seat, and would have liked our positions to have been reversed, but, wishing to gain all the information I could from him, commenced conversation by telling him of the annoyance I had been exposed to at the Pyramids, and how little I had seen there in consequence. Whereupon he gave me his card, bearing his name and address (the Mena Hotel), telling me that I only had to show that to be able to wander about where I liked unmolested.

In spite of my undignified position, we managed to keep up a conversation till we arrived at the Museum (just then moved from Cairo to half-way between Cairo and the Pyramids). By that time I felt that I had had enough of the company of the son of the Sheik, and fondly hoped to find that he had mounted his horse and left when I returned from visiting the Museum; but no such luck. He was waiting for me, so I seated myself inside the victoria and signalled to him to sit on the boxseat, and so we entered Cairo! He begged to serve as my guide during the short time I had left to see something of Cairo, but having already engaged the driver of the victoria, I had to decline the Sheik's offer, and I saw no more of him.

About four years ago I took a passage in the Stella Polaris, a Norwegian steamer hired by a Swedish Travel Bureau to make trips up the Black Sea, touching at interesting places on the way and giving facilities for passengers to land at different ports to make inland trips. I think it was at Haifa where I landed and went by motor to Jerusalem, and from there by train to Cairo. On that occasion I revisited the Pyramids. About one hundred passengers from the Stella Polaris were at the Mena Hotel, where it was arranged for us to have our tea on our return from the Pyramids. From the Mena Hotel to the Pyramids we had the choice of riding camels or donkeys or driving in little go-carts drawn by donkeys – I chose a camel, although I was probably the oldest in the party (eighty-three years of age). We were told to muster at the Sphinx, and our whole time was spent in posing for a photograph, and then all the party, excepting myself, returned to the hotel to tea. I made a detour and arrived at the hotel when the tea was over. I took it for granted that we were all going inside the big pyramid, and was surprised when our Swedish guide told me that no one intended to go. He kindly got me some tea and engaged a nice old Arab, who drove one of the little go-carts, to drive me up to the entrance of the galleries of the Great Pyramid and also told him I was not to be asked for baksheesh.

On the way I asked my Arab driver if the son of the Sheik of the Pyramids, who had given me his card so many years before, was still living, and showed him the card. The old man told me that he was dead, but that he was a relation of his, and that he had known him well. At the entrance of the Great Pyramid two young Arabs took charge of me and conducted me through the galleries into the chambers, one walking in front of me and the other behind. So at last I was able to see the galleries and chambers, but was sorry not to see the son of the Sheik. The two Arabs once stopped for rest, but I ordered them to proceed, as I was not tired. They also asked me for baksheesh and tried to miss some of the galleries, but I held my own and insisted on seeing all. It was such a hurried visit, there was no time to take in all the wonderful sights; what I did see and can remember, though only five or six years ago, has already become a beautiful dream.

I must now return to my first visit to the Pyramids. The rest of the day was spent in seeing all there was time for in Cairo. I left by a late train to meet the Captain of the tramp on a certain wharf at a prearranged time. It was quite dark when the train from Cairo reached Alexandria.

I had learned only a few words of Arabic which I hoped would be enough to direct the driver of the carriage whom I engaged on leaving the train to take me to the wharf. But unfortunately the driver took me to the wharf where the P&O boats started from, and there he left me. The place was badly lit; there was nowhere I could make enquiries. There were a few men about, but they were unable to help me. I wandered about, hoping to find someone who would or could help me, but in vain. For once I thought myself fairly stranded, when suddenly I caught sight of a heap of stones which I had noticed when the Captain had landed me on the previous day. I hardly knew how to express my feelings of relief when I at length found the tramp. The Captain was getting anxious, as it was past the appointed time for our meeting, and he was accustomed to my always being punctual. We soon got on board and the anchor was weighed.

Our next stopping place was Jaffa, then the chief landing place for travellers to Jerusalem. Our stay at Jaffa did not give me time enough to visit Jerusalem. The Captain allowed me to land with him. The tramp was out in the roadstead a good distance from shore and the sea was rather rough. To enable me to get into the shore-boat alongside the tramp, I had to hold on to a rope and at the word "Let go," given when the boat was on the crest of a wave, I did so, and dropped into the arms of Arabs extended for my reception.

This was not at all an uncommon way of landing at Jaffa in those days. The approach to the shore was very rocky, and the boat rowed by the Arabs wound its way between the rocks and landed us at the wharf. The Captain told me to watch for the signal to join the ship. He could not allow me much time on shore, as he had a valuable cargo of sesamum[5] seed on deck which must not get wet, and the sea might get rougher any moment. I had just time to visit the so-called House of Simon the Tanner and secure some oranges before it was time to return to the tramp. The Jaffa oranges, always renowned, were then thin skinned, quite different from those now cultivated by Jews in Palestine.

At Jaffa, and at ports after leaving, there many deck passengers came on board: Turks, Jews, and Arabs. They sorted themselves and camped down in the well of the steamer. It was interesting to watch them from the upper deck, especially in the early morning, when they were performing their toilets in their own curious manner.

At one place of call in Syria I was allowed a long day on shore, and wandered with my butterfly net well into the country. I halted at midday in a vineyard where the grapes were enormous; huge bunches were lying on the ground, the vines not being able to bear their weight. It reminded me of a picture I had seen in an illustrated Bible depicting the story in Numbers xiii. 23: "And they came unto the brook of Eshcol, and cut down from thence a branch with one cluster of grapes, and they bare it

---

5. Sesame

between two upon a staff". I took my meal Arab fashion, seated with the workers in the vineyard round a huge shallow iron pot containing the food, which was a kind of batter with lumps of meat in it. The natives ate with their fingers, picking out bits that they fancied. I used my spoon and fork, which I always carried with me in readiness for such emergencies, and secured a portion before it was fingered.

At Alexandria a pleasant young Italian came on board. He and I landed together at Alexandretta, but found our separate ways to the market, where we went to buy our luncheon. On meeting outside the market, we found we had each filled our baskets with the same provisions, namely Arab bread, olives, and grapes. We then followed the main road out of the town. On each side of the road was a dirty smelly ditch and a noise like "flop, flop" which we found was caused by tortoises tumbling into the water at our approach. We transferred our luncheon into one basket, so as to put some tortoises in the other. We caught them with my butterfly net. On the outskirts of the town we rashly picked and ate prickly pears, with the result that we had to scrape the prickles off each other's face with our penknives.

The country when we reached it was not at all inviting. Under the shade of a solitary pomegranate tree we sat down and ate our luncheon, disturbed by the tortoises getting out of their basket and trying to escape. We turned them over on their backs, but they poked their heads out and righted themselves. We came to the conclusion that we had many more than we wanted, and decided that we would just take four on board, one for each officer; so we let the rest escape. I soon had to regret the capture of those tortoises, as on arrival on board, the steward could think of no other receptacle in which to keep them than the bath, and from that time on it was unusable.

We touched at Beirut. I had an introduction to the Lady Superior of a very High Church Mission. She took me for a drive to the spot where St. George is supposed to have killed the dragon, and to a beautiful grove of stately Lebanon cedars, now almost exterminated. On a great height there is a Government reserve where there are a few young Lebanon cedars.

From one point I took the train to Ephesus to visit the ruins. Before starting, the station master gave me Turkish coffee and seemed very troubled in his mind that I should think of visiting the ruins alone. At length he insisted on sending a man with me, who would see that I was not molested. The man kept at a respectful distance the whole time. I never saw a living creature during the whole excursion, and cannot imagine why the station master should have been alarmed on my account.

The next port of importance we stopped at was Smyrna, where we made a stay of several days, and where I came in contact with Armenians. The tramp was moored alongside the wharf, where there was always a smart dragoman who pestered to be my guide whenever I landed. I declined his services till the last day. The first day I made my way into the town and enquired for the

Armenian quarters. To get there I had to pass through the Jewish and Turkish quarters. Most of the house doors were open, and women were sitting in the doorways, all glad to have a chat. Of course we spoke French.

In the Armenian quarter a lady asked me into her house, saying that she thought I looked tired. I accepted gladly, and she took me into a nice sitting-room. The first impression was of great cleanliness, as there were white linen covers over all the furniture. She regaled me on the usual Turkish coffee while I sat and rested on the sofa. When I thought it was time to leave she begged me to stay on, and her maid soon brought in a tray on which were several different kinds of preserves, a handsome silver bowl containing spoons, and another bowl filled with water in which to deposit the spoon after it had been used. I found that I was expected to sample every preserve. My hostess was very guarded in her conversation, avoiding all allusion to politics or the Turks. I think that her object in inviting me to stay on so long was more to ascertain where I had come from and all about my travels than anything else, and I on my part was glad of the rest.

My next encounter with the Armenians was when making a visit to the tomb, or what is believed to be the tomb, of an early Christian bishop. This tomb is situated about two miles from Smyrna in the mountains. There was a well-worn path, and on it I overtook a party of Armenians on their way to visit the tomb, so I joined them. When we reached the tomb we found it surrounded by Turkish soldiers, whose manners were very rude towards the Armenians. The tomb itself was in charge of a Turkish woman. A green turban was on the tomb, which the Turks were claiming as being that of a Moslem saint. I noticed that the Armenians were very much afraid of the Turkish soldiers. One Armenian got to the side of the tomb, where, unobserved, he snatched a twig of the cypress tree which was over-growing the tomb and gave it to me. On leaving the tomb we made a wide circuit to gain our downward path so as to avoid passing the Turkish soldiers again.

On our return to Smyrna, one of the Armenian ladies invited me to her house. I found she belonged to the mercantile class – her house was behind a large warehouse. As always happened when in company with the Armenians, they carefully avoided all allusion to politics in their conversation. I was given the usual coffee, and then I bade farewell.

There was a charming English lady living near the wharf in charge of the Sailors Home. The Captain took me to the Home and introduced me to her. She sent her dragoman with me whenever I wanted to make a purchase, to ensure my not being cheated. I shall never forget the cantaloupe melon he selected for me.

The smart dragoman who always waylaid me whenever I landed at the wharf had come down in his prices. He offered to act as my guide for one franc a day, and he promised to take me to see a slave market if I engaged him. I engaged him conditionally, "No slave market, no one franc." He took me through many winding narrow streets till I think he thought I had lost my bearings;

he then pointed out a square where he said the slaves were put up for auction. I asked where the slaves were, and he pointed to a warehouse with large high doors. I looked through a crack in the door, and saw nothing but figs piled up inside. I turned round and smiled at him. Then he said they were away on the mountains, had been taken up there for exercise. He was evidently beginning to fear he would not get his franc.

He then took me to a warehouse where figs were being flattened out and packed in boxes for export to England and other countries. Since visiting that warehouse I have avoided pulled figs. My basket was filled with figs, not pulled ones, but I was not allowed to pay for them. As I considered I had got my money's worth, I told my dragoman that if he would take me by the nearest way to the Museum, which I wanted to visit again, he should have his franc, although he had not taken me to the slave market.

The Curator of the Museum wanted me to effect an exchange of a piece of Greek statuary with the British Museum, but the transaction did not come off, as the piece wanted by the Curator of the Smyrna Museum was lost at sea.

Before leaving England I was given an introduction to a gentleman in Smyrna who had a Greek wife. She offered to take me to see a Turkish harem. I regretted later that I did not accompany her. My refusal was owing to my travelstained garments, although she assured me it did not signify, as the ladies of the harem would not notice my attire, but only take pleasure in showing off their Parisian garments. She also told me that the Pashas were beginning to curtail the number of their wives, owing to the expense of having to send to Paris for their robes.

The Captain had expressed a wish to have a dog that would help to keep down the rats with which the ship was infested. When we were going on board just before leaving, one of the sailors, who had overheard the Captain's desire for a dog, seized one that was on the wharf and brought it on board. The wharf and the ship were very dimly lighted, and we could not see what the dog was like, only that he was not very large and white. We were delighted to have a pet on board, and did all in our power to make friends with it. The Captain, surmising that it might have fleas, ordered the steward to give it a bath. The steward nearly wept, saying the dog would not like him if he washed it. By daylight we were well out at sea, making for the Grecian Islands. The dog proved to be a most hideous mongrel, dachshund prevailing in its breed. A veritable cur! The sight of the first rat made it bolt with its tail between its legs. All on board turned against the dog and wanted to throw it overboard. With difficulty I persuaded the Captain to let me keep it till it could be put ashore. We soon sighted a small island, and the Captain had a boat lowered, into which I got and was rowed to the island, where I landed the dog. We stopped at some of the Grecian Islands, and afterwards made our way to Patras to get a cargo of currants (dried), of which the place reeked.

I was allowed time to go on shore to visit Olympia. The agents of the tramp would insist on sending one of their clerks with me, telling me he would not be any expense to me, as his mother lived in the town to which I had to go by train, and that he would stay with her for the night. I stayed at a cheap but quite comfortable hotel, and in the morning, on giving an elderly chambermaid a small tip, she raised and kissed the hem of my dress to show her gratitude. To expedite matters, I paid my bill, before the young clerk appeared, in coin. When he came, he was quite annoyed, as he wished and intended to pay it in paper, which would have been of less value.

The journey was by carriage, the one we hired being a sort of barouche drawn by a pair of lean horses. On the previous day, in conversation, the clerk had told me that he had a young sister of whom he was very fond, and I told him to bring her with him when we went to Olympia. On going to the carriage at the door of the hotel, I was disagreeably surprised to see a fat and elderly lady inside the barouche. This uninvited guest was the young man's mother. His little sister was on the box with him, where I should have liked to have been instead of inside with the fat, uninteresting lady, with whom I had nothing in common. Her extra weight was probably the cause of the half-starved horses making very slow progress over the bad roads.

When we arrived at Olympia there was little time for exploring, and, of course, the fat old lady could not move quickly. We had to catch a train at the town where we had spent the night, but the slowness of our progress caused us to miss it. But the last of the goods trains, containing nothing but currants, was just starting when we arrived at the station, and a carriage was connected for the clerk and myself in which we returned to Patras. All was hurry and scurry on board, as the cargo of currants had to be loaded and discharged as quickly as possible at Marseilles before a tariff, which was shortly coming into force, was due. We got to Marseilles in time to save the duty on the currants. From there we crossed the Mediterranean to Algiers. We had about the roughest passage across that it was possible to have, and I was too sea-sick to care what happened to me. When next I saw the Captain, he said we had been in imminent danger of being wrecked, partly caused by the water tanks having become displaced.

From Algiers the tramp had orders to proceed to New York. That order caused dismay among the officers. As a matter of form, they had signed on for two years, but they were not expecting to be sent beyond the Mediterranean. By the time they were due to arrive in New York it would be mid-winter, and they were not provided with warm clothing. What was available of my outfit for Armenia I turned to account for them. My revolver and cartridges I sold to the fourth officer. I left the tramp at Algiers, intending to remain there till the spring, but I found a letter waiting for me from England, telling me my father was very ill, so I decided to go straight home. I saw the Captain and officers again and asked if I could do anything for them in England, as they would be away so much longer than they expected. The Captain and the first officer were glad to give me commissions.

The Captain, finding himself in a position to get married, asked me to find out if a girl he had fixed his affections on was still free, and if so, whether she had any kindly feelings towards him. She lived with her family at Clapham. When he had last heard of them they were thinking of emigrating to Australia. If in Australia, he wished me to find out their address from a neighbour in Clapham.

The first officer requested me to redeem a valuable watch which he had been driven to pledge at Attenborough's in the Strand to enable him to buy his outfit. The watch had been pledged for £2. He gave me the pawn ticket and wanted to give me the £2, but that I declined. The third officer was "very sad; he had been married just before starting on this trip. He thought he was only going for a short cruise in the Mediterranean. He had no commission to give me. The fourth officer had married in haste and was repenting at leisure! He had married very young, was spending money in employing detectives to watch his wife, and hoped to get sufficient evidence for a separation; as he was a Roman Catholic he could not get a divorce.

On arriving home, I carried out my commissions. The young lady had left Clapham for Australia, and her friends believed she was still unmarried. I communicated the result of my enquiries to the Captain, but heard no more. If he received my letter, I hope he communicated in time with his lady love, otherwise he would probably have found she was married, as eligible girls were then scarce in Australia and soon picked up.

The first officer's watch was redeemed for me by a nephew of mine. As it was a valuable one we decided to keep it until we could hand it over to its owner in person, although a professed friend of his wanted to pay the redemption money and take care of the watch for him. The owner returned to England sooner than we had anticipated. While in New York he had met with an accident. The fourth officer was practising with the revolver he had bought from me and shot the first officer through the stomach. He was laid up in hospital in New York and made a marvellous recovery. As soon as he was able, he returned to England. My nephew who had redeemed the watch, and was a doctor, handed it over to him and told me that, although still looking far from well, he was recovering rapidly from the effects of the accident.

The massacre of the Armenians by the Turks took place in October 1886. I only heard of it on my arrival in London. I wrote to the Armenians I had previously been in correspondence with, also to the clergyman who held the fund, which I had not used, to redeem my promise to tell them what I had found out about the ill-treatment of the Armenians by the Turks. In reply I was requested to take the fund and if possible find my way into Armenia to verify the accounts of the massacre; so far the Turks had prevented anyone penetrating into the country.

My father beseeched me not to go on any more wild travels during his lifetime, and I had hardly time to decide what to do when news came that newspaper correspondents had found their way into Armenia, and they were able, of course, to give a better account of what had taken place than I could have done. The whole tragic story soon appeared in the English press.

Many years later, when cycling in Scotland, I made friends with a lady in Edinburgh, who, like myself, was a keen cyclist, and when I was leaving her house she accompanied me part of the way. I happened to have with me the address of the clergyman who held the Armenian fund and asked her if she knew him. "He is a great friend of mine, and we shall be passing his house," she replied. We called on him. He was glad to have my personal account of what I had been able to learn about the treatment of the Armenians.

He told me he found the Armenians were most unsatisfactory to deal with, and the fund had gone to assist those who had escaped to Cyprus, which island England had allowed to be used as a refuge.

CHAPTER VIII
CYCLING EUROPE, 1894

AS soon as sunk frames came in for bicycles, in 1894, I took up cycling, and found it a cheap and ideal way of travelling. My first cycle was a child's "Townsend," which was ridden to bits by the time I returned from my first trip to Italy. I took it to the shop where I bought it and asked to have it replaced by the best cycle they had, which was a "Singer Grand Modéle de Luxe," and I was allowed the £7 I had given for the little "Townsend." After I had ridden the "Singer" 10,000 miles, I took it to the makers at Coventry. They put it into thorough order, making no charge. I told them I should be going to Italy again, which interested them, so I sent them a card from Syracuse in Sicily. From that time Singers always changed my cycle whenever there was a proved improvement in their machine. On two or three occasions they exhibited the discarded cycle in the window of their London showroom on Holborn Viaduct with an account of the mileage. It was put into the window, mud and all!

In the early days of cycling, soon after pneumatic tyres had come in, Sir Benjamin Richardson started a club for bicyclists and tricyclists, of which I became a member. We went for rides every Saturday afternoon. We did not cover great distances, as the tricyclists did not get over the ground quickly, but we mustered at appointed places in the country, generally at an old country inn, for tea. During the summer we put up at some interesting place for a few days and made excursions. I well remember an excursion to Winchester, where we were hospitably received and entertained by the Mayor and others. The Mayor regaled us on strawberries and cream in the room over the old gate in the town. In return for hospitalities received, the members of the club gave a dinner at the hotel where we stayed, and being the senior lady of the club, I was asked to select a gentleman guest to take me in to dinner. My choice rested between the Mayor and the Bursar of Winchester School, whose acquaintance I had made, for he had shown us round and entertained us at the School. I selected the Bursar.

Sir Benjamin and Lady Richardson, at that time living in Manchester Square, were old friends, and I missed no opportunity of attending their Sunday afternoon "At Homes," on which occasions one was sure to meet interesting people.

The first I ever heard of Mormons was on meeting members of the Hepworth Dixon family there. Whether Hepworth Dixon's book giving an account of Brigham Young's wonderful trek to Utah was written before or after my meeting them I cannot remember, but years later, on visiting Salt Lake City, I realised what a wonderful trek it was, and what privations Brigham Young and his followers must have endured.

Having spent so many hours with, and retaining such pleasant recollections of, Sir Benjamin Richardson and his family, I feel I must say a little about them. There were two sons and one daughter. I can only recall the younger son to my memory. He was full of fun and very witty. Both brothers made great game of their sister when she became engaged to a curate who happened to be tall and lanky – they called him "Stella's Fire Escape." The younger son was a sculptor, but gave up Art to devote himself to his father, who was then so well known in the scientific world. He was a great authority on the subject of hygiene and alcoholism; he himself was a total abstainer. His latter days were devoted to perfecting his invention of the lethal chamber for putting unwanted animals to death in a merciful manner. The daughter recently lost her husband.

Singers presented me with a lovely bicycle listed at thirty-eight guineas. It was a perfect dream to ride, but shortly afterwards they asked for its return, as they had perfected the free-wheel and wished me to have one. That free-wheel was very heavy, and I was not sorry when it came to grief; I was knocked over by a heavy van on Kingston Bridge. I was unhurt, but the bicycle was ruined. I got no redress, as, although I noticed the name of the van, the driver denied being on the bridge at the

The author's nephew, Walter Pemberton Fooks, M.D

time of the accident. I sent the debris to Coventry and got another machine at a reduced price. Singers always built especially for me, as I required a small but strongly built machine.

As soon as I learned to cycle, I rode with my two nephews, medical students, on a tour round the coast of Devonshire and Cornwall, hugging the coast, and avoiding the high roads, which we found unpleasant, as cycling was quite a novelty, especially for women, and we received too much attention from dogs and factory and mill girls. I was fifty years of age when I commenced to cycle, and I cycled till my eightieth year.

The first year I rode over 13,000 miles, the second over 12,000 and for many following years 10,000 each. The first few years were mostly devoted to England, Scotland and Ireland, and on the Continent to Germany, France, and Italy. My great mistake was riding such long distances at a stretch, every day intending to do sixty miles or more. I suppose it was having begun what seemed to me an ideal way of travelling so late in life. I wanted to see all I could of the world, but really passed by much of interest in my anxiety to get over the ground, and when I did halt at places of interest, I was generally too tired to look round. I did not then know I was going to live to my eighty-ninth year and still retain my activity and love of travel and adventure.

Since giving up cycling, I have travelled in countries where I could not cycle, and now I am able to travel in a more leisurely way.

As I had a low-geared cycle, I generally started before my nephews got up, and we usually arranged to meet at some place for luncheon. A village near Bideford was one stopping-place. I arrived there and waited in vain for my nephews. I grew anxious about them, and rode back to Bideford, feeling sure that there must have been some accident. I enquired for the best cycle shop, and there I recognised my nephews' cycles. The cycle belonging to the younger one was under repair; he had come into collision with Bideford Bridge. I traced my nephews to Westward Ho! We spent the night at Bideford, and the next morning we all started off together. The injured cycle did not run so well as before the accident, and we had to stop continually for more repairs, none of which was satisfactory; also the boy was knocked up – he was not very robust – so he trained back to London, and his brother and I pursued our journey, still hugging the coast. But the delay on account of the accident necessitated his leaving me to finish the journey alone. He left me at Charmouth and rode back to London at the rate of 100 miles a day.

I was no sooner back in London myself than I started for France to stay with friends – Dr. and Mrs. Baraduc and their two sons, living at Montaigut en Combrailles in the Puy de Dôme Mountains. I arrived, having cycled all the way through France. The two sons were then at home for their holidays. Without resting, I immediately started on a cycling tour with them. The elder boy was studying for the legal profession, and has risen to the top of the tree. The younger was studying medicine, and is now practising during the season at Châtelguyon, an inland watering place in the Puy de Dôme Mountains, consisting mostly of fashionable hotels, at that time the practice of his uncle. We spent a few days there.

Dr. Baraduc of Montaigut en Combrailles was the doctor to the Saint Eloi coal-mines. Both he and his brother in Châtelguyon and their wives are now dead.

It was very hot weather when we left Montaigut at three o'clock in the morning for Châtelguyon. I had not had time to rest and recover from my previous ride with my nephews and the ride to Montaigut. My young French companions were quite fresh and not even tired when we arrived at Châtelguyon, but I was very weary. We arrived in time for dejeuner, and I had to put in an appearance in my soiled cycling costume. The French ladies present must have been astonished, but I suppose attributed my appearance to the usual eccentricities of the English!

Afterwards I rode on to the Riviera, via Nîmes and Arles. A few hours sufficed to see all there was of interest in Nîmes. I had some chocolate while seated in the open in the "Jardin des Fontaines" with the ruins of the Temple of Diana and Roman baths in full view. The old tower above is said by some to have once served as a lighthouse, and there was a good deal of strong evidence in support of the theory. I mounted my bicycle and soon left the long avenue of plane trees behind. The country is not picturesque, being rather flat and lacking timber; the mountains in the distance were too far off to form a good background.

The road to Arles was perfect for cycling. At Arles there were still more Roman remains to be visited. The Arena was perhaps the most interesting, being less restored. In the place of ruined Roman baths were good modern ones, the use of which and a good dinner and a night's rest gave me a fair start on the following morning. I really should not have taken a bath directly on my arrival, as I did, for I had been battling with a head wind from Nimes, but it was so tempting! While in the bath I was overcome with faintness, but hopped out just in time to lie on the cold marble floor, where I soon recovered.

After Arles the roads are still almost level to Marseilles, but the country assumes a different aspect. There is plenty of vegetation, and the distant mountains form a grand background. From there the beautiful scenery commences. It is very varied. One moment there is the luxurious semitropical vegetation of the plains, and suddenly the rugged defiles of the mountains surround you, revealing panoramic views from the roads on their heights. All was beautiful. If one place seemed more beautiful than another, it was perhaps because it happened to be bathed in sunshine.

From Arles to the Toulon side of Marseilles is only a comfortable day's ride, about sixty miles, the roads being extremely good. The disagreeable suburbs of Marseilles may be avoided by training, as I was informed many cyclists did.

Soon after leaving Marseilles there is a choice of roads. I, being a good walker and more in search of the picturesque than intent on long distances, selected the road over the mountains. It involved about twenty miles of uphill work, the hills being, as is usual in France on main roads, of so low a gradient that riding and walking alternately became easy. The highest point being reached, the run down is splendid. Shortly before leaving the mountains and emerging near Toulon, the defiles become grander and grander, the extremely rugged and varied hued rocks being enhanced by vegetation. At Toulon, as at Marseilles, you can go by train through the suburbs, but Toulon is by no means an unpleasant town to ride through.

From Toulon to Hyères is an easy run. Within a few miles of the latter place the smell of violets and the hedges covered with roses reminded me that summer weather was found again, even if the perpetual sunshine from Nîmes had not dispelled all disagreeable recollections of the November frosts and fogs so recently left behind in England. But alas! No roses without thorns! Mosquitoes at Hyères were also rejoicing in the prolonged summer; their ravages had given the inmates of the hotel the appearance of suffering from some epidemic. I, as are all new-comers, was fiercely attacked, and, until proving the efficacy of "Fidibus anti-moustiques," did not get any rest. Although the fumes do not kill, they stupefy the little beasts for some hours. After having had the roads to myself as far as lady cyclists were concerned, it was pleasant to find some at Hyères and to have companions at times for exploring the neighbourhood.

Another week of perpetual sunshine made one forget that it could rain in the South of France. On the day I had fixed for my departure there was a cloudy sky and slight drizzle. The rain was not serious, but had been so a few miles from Hyères, rendering the roads very heavy and travelling tiring. Nightfall came on and I had only reached Le Muy instead of Fréjus. The exterior of the one and only hotel looked unpromising, but the interior proved otherwise, and provided quite a nice little dinner and comfortable bed – all one wants after a hard day on heavy roads with no refreshment but bread and sheep's milk, the latter very nasty, I thought!

I started again almost before daybreak to allow for a short stay at Fréjus, where the old Roman Arena is close to the road and is in itself a good bicycling ground. The curious old Roman quay, still with its iron rings to which the galleys were attached, in my ignorance, I missed seeing. I was told that it is now far inland, owing to the receding of the sea. The viaducts were in full view from the road leading to the Esterels, which had to be crossed before Cannes or my next stopping place, Nice, could be reached.

Sunshine did not favour the Esterels, although a few gleams appeared as I reached the highest point and the beautiful view of the sea and St. Raphael appeared in sight where the road bent. The run down to Cannes is splendid. It was raining there, so I was delayed, and found the roads very heavy between there and Nice. I was looking forward to the comforts of my portmanteau and good quarters in Nice, but that pleasant prospect had to be given up for inferior accommodation which I obtained at Cagnes, about twelve miles distant.

Early next morning I covered the twelve miles to Nice before a real downpour came on which lasted for two days. The week intended for the sights of Nice stretched into a fortnight, still far too short a time to do justice to its environs. A more lovely cycling centre for those able to combine walking and riding, it would be difficult to find. There are numerous good roads through the mountains, all leading to somewhere worth visiting. I found it often difficult to learn from the peasants where the roads led to. Their ideas do not extend far beyond their homes, and their measure of distance is according to the pace they walk! Through Grasse and round by Cannes was a lovely ride; also that up the valley of the Var to Puget-Theniers and back to Nice over the mountains from St. Martin and down the St. Andre valley.

With great regret I was forced to leave Nice, having determined to bicycle round the whole of the French and Italian Riviera. I enjoyed perfect weather the whole fortnight I spent in Nice, but on the day of my departure a "Tramontana" set in. The heat having been rather oppressive for cycling, the "Tramontana" cooled the air, and finding it would be at my back, I decided to start and let myself be blown to Bordighera. At times the gusts accompanied by clouds of dust were overpowering, and I had to seek refuge under any available shelter. As the wind was very high and anticipated troubles at the Italian frontier were before me, I took the lower and shorter road.

The beautiful Corniche road between Nice and Cap St. Martin are too well known to mention. The frontier troubles I will not dwell on. My French Cyclists' Touring Club ticket was quite useless in Italy; not only was the 42 lire duly exacted, but also another 21.85c. for what I never understood, unless it was for adorning my bicycle with a little bit of stamped lead. At the French frontier my bicycle was similarly adorned, but no charge was made, and it was done with great civility whereas in Italy civility was conspicuous by its absence. One and a half hours' delay made me late at Bordighera, where I arrived to find that my portmanteau had not been forwarded from Ventimiglia, nor was I able to get it for two days, in spite of profuse promises of quick delivery.

Immediately on crossing the frontier, the inferiority of Italian roads became apparent; also the street boys were very rude. They threw stones in front of my bicycle. These small troubles, added to the delay at the frontier, gave such an unpleasant impression of Italy as a bicycling ground for a lady alone that even Bordighera, with all its beauties and pleasant English society, failed to please me.

A few attempts at exploring the neighbourhood off the main roads had to be given up out of respect for my bicycle tyres. So I turned my back on Bordighera, to find by experience that cycling in Italy, at all events in winter, involves a great amount of walking. Road-mending there consisted of shovelling rough stones onto the roads and leaving them for the traffic to wear down. The roads are not so well engineered as in France, the gradients being much higher. Consequently, progress was of necessity slow, but not to be regretted on that account, as it allowed time to admire the lovely scenery. The sun was a little overpowering about noon when the shade of an olive tree was welcome.

The peasants I passed on the road were most pleasant and genial. Alassio was a short run from Bordighera, and I arrived there early in the afternoon. The town looked inviting, so I gave up all idea of making for Finale Marina, which was to have been my next stopping place, on account of the interesting caves and Neolithic remains there. I only passed through the following day, and decided that I had done well to stop at Alassio.

At Alvengo there is a fine old Roman bridge, and as it is close to the road and far away from the present river bed, it cannot fail to draw attention. The outward appearance of the villages seemed clean. Fishing was apparently the chief occupation. At Savona, making the rough pottery used by the French and Italian peasants seemed the chief industry. As one approached the town, the wayside was lined with "cruches" and domestic utensils, drying in the sun.

The suburbs of Genoa began at Pigli, and as the "Tramontana" was again blowing, it was not an agreeable prospect. I was advised to take the train, and was told that my bicycle would attract unpleasant attention. The stretch of level road was too great a treat and novelty to miss, and the "Tramontana" deprived me of all attention from street idlers, as their energy was entirely devoted to keeping on or running after their hats and blowing on their fingers when out of their pockets to keep them warm. A very little cold damps the ardour and enthusiasm of an Italian street boy.

The most beautiful part of the Italian Riviera is considered to commence after Genoa from Nervi to Spezia. The attractions of Nervi proved so great that I could not make an early start. I expected bad roads and heeded a warning not to attempt the lonely road over the mountains from Cestri to Spezia without six good hours of daylight. I left Nervi, only intending to go as far as Sestri, but the roads were wonderfully good, and a quick run had become a novelty. I made only short halts, just to ask the way and examine patterns of lace made by women sitting at their doors with lace pillows on their laps, I was so determined not to waste any time.

At 12.30 p.m. I reached Sestri, the most uninviting place I had passed since I left Nervi. The temptation to go on was great. The caution not to proceed had come from a German tricyclist, who seemed to have a vague idea of distances, so I decided to go on. I did not stop for luncheon, as I had a piece of bread and an apple in my pocket. I started on the uphill journey as fast as the broiling sun and the unavoidable halts to admire the scenery would allow me. I washed down my dry bread with refreshing draughts from wayside springs. After about two hours of steady uphill work, I spied some objects ahead which proved to be a man and his wife and family with a mule carrying what was probably all their worldly belongings.

I enquired how far it was to Spezia. "Seven hours a piedi," was his reply. As I had lately overtaken him and was now leaving him behind, his "a piedi" would not be my "a piedi," if I could combine it with occasional rides. A level piece of road was in view. I felt cheered and expected to cover the ground "a bicycle." But alas! The road was all stones and had to be walked. Then came another ascent, which must have been to the highest point, as there alone icicles were hanging from the rocks and glistening in the sunshine.

At length I had a good level run and there were some villages in sight. I tried to get some milk, but it seemed to be unheard of. I could not spare the time to wait for boiling water for making tea, which I had with me. The wine I was able to procure had a most unpleasant taste and smell, but I drank what I could, bought some more bread, and started off again without getting much information about the road.

Soon, road-mending – or rather stone-spreading – again stopped my riding. Road-menders in France and Italy had often given me the only reliable information as to distance that I could get, so I felt sure that the "about twenty miles" given in this instance was not far out. It was then past three o'clock, and all idea of reaching Spezia before dark had to be abandoned. There was a good road before me and some downhill work, which was a pleasant change. Then came another but shorter hill and a level road again, and then darkness, and that before even getting a view of Spezia from the mountains.

The descent seemed too steep and the curves too dangerous to attempt riding. Also there was considerable mule-cart and foot traffic on the road, showing that Spezia could not be very far off. The peasants wished me a pleasant "Good night" as I passed them. The stars came out, it was a lovely night, and I was fully enjoying it all when my meditations were brought to an abrupt end by a challenge from the sentry at the gate of Spezia. On discovering that I was a woman, his astonishment was only equalled by his civility.

A postman passed just as I was asking the sentry to direct me to a hotel, and he took me in charge. I tried hard to be pleasant to him, but in an unknown language the result was not good. The paved streets of Spezia seemed to me never ending. It made me speculate on the number of miles I must have walked and to realise how dreadfully tired I was. At last we reached the hotel. The joy I felt was great. My conductor would not accept a tip, so we just shook hands and said "Good night." Although it was only 7 p.m., it seemed much later, it was so long after sunset.

The next day I decided that Carrara was worthy of a deviation from the main road. The sight of the quarries did not repay the delay and consequent wet finish to my journey. It is a place spoiled by tourists and the one place where I found any inclination to dishonesty. To make the most of my time there I allowed myself to become the prey of a perfectly unnecessary guide, who afterwards demanded more than three times the price agreed upon, on the plea that he had taken me farther up the mountain than the tourists usually go. His extortions were backed up by my landlord, who could easily have directed me to follow the railway, which was all the information necessary for one going to the quarries. They are worked in a most primitive way.

On trundling my cycle up a hill near Carrara, I was rather startled by a big man coming towards me leading a small donkey in a small cart. He rushed across the road and seized hold of my cycle. My alarm vanished on looking up at his face, which beamed with good nature. He had never seen a cycle before, and he wanted me to mount. I was able to muster enough Italian to explain that the road was too bad and the hill too steep. For miles in the vicinity of Carrara the roads are about as bad as they possibly could be. A wet night made them impossible for riding. I attempted twice, and twice I had side-slips, with disastrous results to my garments. I had to stop at wayside inns to dry and brush them.

After Pietra and Santa, the road leaves the mountains and follows the valley of the Arno. It is a good road, but with high banks and a ditch each side and with the exception of the few miles that it passes through a pine forest, it is not picturesque. Through the pine forest the Duomo and Baptistery of Pisa soon appeared in sight, lighted up by the reflection of a most glorious but wild sunset, giving little promise of improved weather.

Another night's rain made riding again quite impossible, so I started in good time, trundling my bicycle and hoping for sunshine to mend matters. Between walking and riding, but mostly walking, I only got as far as Empoli by nightfall, and the best had to be made of the poor accommodation it offered, as it had come on to rain hard and it was impossible to go any farther. I arrived so wet at Empoli that, although it was only afternoon, I had to go to bed to allow my clothes to be dried. I asked the landlord to let me have a book to read. The only book he possessed was Robinson Crusoe in French, and he was trying to teach himself French with it.

From Empoli I got a dry start, but had to walk for some miles before riding was possible; then the roads so far improved that the foundations were sound, and by avoiding ruts I found it possible to ride through slush till at length I reached Porta Romana. Beyond a few stones thrown at my bicycle near Hyères, I did not meet with any more rudeness from the inhabitants. Of course, in villages where lady cyclists had never been seen before, I attracted a great deal of attention, but it was quite friendly. In England, during my early cycling days, I have met with more unpleasant notice than either in France or Italy, and hitherto have found the two latter countries more pleasant to ride alone in, and also slightly less expensive.

Once, on arrival at a country inn in France, which I had previously sampled and found comfortable and extremely moderate in price, I was disappointed to find it already beset by a rather rowdy wedding party. I had counted on spending the night there, but under the circumstances I just partook of some coffee and remounted my cycle. The wit of the party – I think it was the bridegroom –

called out, "Madame, vous avez une roue qui tourne," and I replied, "Oui, Monsieur, j'ai même deux roues qui tournent," much to his astonishment and I think to the increased merriment of the guests, who laughed loudly at his expense!

Cycling on a very muddy road in England, I politely asked a man who was leading a horse in a farm cart to go to his proper side of the road and allow me to pass. His reply was, "Go to Hell!" But on my saying that I would rather not, as I should meet him there, he went to the right side of the road to allow me to pass. Later in the day I again had to pass him, and he did not repeat his polite remark.

York Road Lying-in Hospital, Lambeth

CHAPTER IX

MIDWIFERY TRAINING, 1897

IN the summer of 1897 I was at the York Road Lying-in Hospital, training to become a midwife. I thought the experience might at some future time be useful to me, as I had no intention of giving up travelling, and there was no knowing when my assistance and knowledge might be welcome. The training was for three months. I was one of six pupils. Lectures were given by the resident midwife. We six pupils had a private sitting room. We had the charge of three lying-in Wards, two pupils to each Ward. We had to do all the work except polishing the floors.

I had engagements which prevented me from attending the first two or three lectures of the course. As I was the last to join, I had no choice in the selection of my fellow worker. I had a bedroom allotted me in the house of the district nurse instead of the hospital with the other pupils. I found my fellow worker very peculiar. Although she had been in domestic service, she neither liked nor could do domestic work. She was anxious to "better" herself.

When we took possession of our Ward, I suggested that we should arrange our work so as not to clash or overlap, to which she seemed to consent, but she followed me round the Ward doing again just what I had done. In many other ways I found her odd, and she got on my nerves. Seeing that she so disliked the cleaning and dusting, I offered to attend to the Ward alone, and she was quite contented. Soon, however, her relations had to be sent for to take her away, for she had periodic fits of madness.

The Ward was quite easy to keep in order, the only drawback being an old-fashioned zinc sink which the doctors frequently stained with their chemicals, and, the funds of the hospital being low, it was a difficult matter to get sufficient cleaning materials to keep it clean and bright. When I did get any I had to hide them, as the nurses who were not supposed to enter the lying-in Wards used to crib them.

I always prided myself upon having my Ward ready for any emergency. There was some competition between the pupils to get the services of the floor-polisher first, so that we could get our cleaning and dusting done before the "doctors' rounds." No one was allowed into the Wards without authority, but mine was often raided by nurses for baby linen, which they extracted from the linen chest, and they often washed their teapots in my bright sink! As I had been complimented by the matron and midwife upon always having my Ward clean and tidy and ready for any emergency, this was a bit mortifying. To me, who had learned how to do housework, and worked so hard in New Zealand, and of late years cycled so much, the work seemed like nothing, in fact I liked it. It was not going to last long enough to become monotonous, and, too, I was keen on learning all I could of anything and everything.

During the first lecture at which I was present, I noticed that one of the pupils kept her notebook out of sight, and before the end of the lecture she put her head down and burst into tears, and said she had not been able to follow the lecture or take many notes. She was a nice young girl, and I was very sorry for her and offered to give her what help I could. I went with her after the lecture to her room and read through with her what notes she had taken. These were really too funny and had the effect of making us both laugh, which cleared the air. In one instance she had written "removed the bowels" instead of "move." I quite enjoyed going through her notes with her after the subsequent lectures, and the repetition also helped me with my work.

Tickets for plays and concerts were often sent to the hospital, for which pupils and nurses drew lots. When Queen Victoria's Diamond Jubilee came round, six tickets were sent for the nurses and an extra one for the Matron, by the Duchess of Buccleuch, for seats erected in her garden to view the procession. I failed to draw a ticket and expected to see the procession from the roof of the Hospital; but when the day arrived, the Matron asked me to use her ticket, as she did not like to leave the Hospital while so many of the nurses were away.

I arrayed myself in my best black silk dress, and was received with the nurses at the entrance gate of the mansion of the Duchess of Buccleuch by a daughter of the Duchess, who presented me with a programme of the procession and showed me the seats allotted to us and told us to make ourselves quite at home; she also said there were light refreshments in the garden and more solid ones in the house.

We took our seats, but the nurses soon left me, preferring to walk about the garden together. As there was time to get some refreshment before the procession was due, I made for the house, thinking a little change of diet would be a treat, for dinner at the Hospital, with only one exception, had been leg of mutton every day, of which I thought at first I would never tire. But the sad and trying cases I had been attending had got on my nerves and taken away my appetite and I had had to keep myself going by indulging in oysters on the way from the Hospital to my night quarters.

The feast in the Duchess's house was a real treat, supplemented by champagne, which flowed freely. The nurses lost a lot by having left me, for they would not venture into the house without me. I regained my seat to view the procession, but beyond a glance at the Queen and her Lady-in-Waiting, the Duchess of Buccleuch, who gave a friendly recognition to us nurses in her garden, my chief interest was in trying to catch sight of the last of the Stuarts riding in the cavalcade of horsemen surrounding the Queen's carriage. I had seen his name in the programme, and was most anxious to see what he was like.

I did my best to get on with the pupils and nurses, but many of them seemed from the first evening of my arrival to take a dislike to me. Probably they were a bit jealous of me. I was of independent means, educated, travelled, and a lady, none of which "faults" could I help having!

I was reading the lines on the hands of one of the pupils when the Matron sent for me and asked me to read her hands, and also those of the head midwife. Palmistry was all the rage at the time, and I had dabbled in it. Probably that was another "fault" that made the pupils and nurses dislike me. I did all I could to be friendly with them. I used to go early to Covent Garden Market to get strawberries and visit a dairy on my way back for cream, on which we all feasted together.

There was one pupil, who was engaged to be married to a medical missionary in China, and she was expecting to go out to him and practise midwifery. I did not keep in touch with her, but in reading her hand the lines told me she was to meet with a violent death. I wonder what became of her.

One of my cases was in the lying-in Ward adjoining the pupils' sitting room. It was late at night, but I could not rest on account of hearing through the walls sounds of the patient's sufferings, and I went in and found the nurse fast asleep. I sent her to bed and watched the case myself. It was a very harrowing case – a young and pretty Irish girl, evidently of good birth. She opened her heart to me, and I gave her as much good advice as was possible under the circumstances.

When the final viva voce examination came off somewhere in Hanover Square, we all passed except poor "Bennie." The doctor who was examining her brought her papers up to the doctor who was questioning me to show them to him, they were so humorous. "Of course, you cannot pass her," was his remark.

Again poor "Bennie" helped me, as her funny papers had taken up the time of the doctors, who might have put awkward questions to me. As it was, when he commenced to "torture" me again, he did all the talking. We had a sad return journey to the Hospital; indeed, I would gladly have passed my certificate on to "Bennie" if it had been possible. However, the Hospital authorities thought so much of her good qualities and felt so sure she would make a good nurse that they kept her on at the Hospital, and eventually she passed the examination.

On receiving my certificate, the district nurse asked me to take on her duties whilst she had a month's holiday, which I consented to do, provided the Hospital authorities agreed. I was also offered a good appointment abroad. Had that chance come in my earlier days when I was so hard up, I would gladly have accepted it. I went through my month's holiday duty, the cases being mostly in the Lower Marsh, Westminster, where there was a great deal of poverty caused by unemployment amongst dock workers. I loved the work, and when leaving, I did so with the intention of taking the month's holiday duty for the midwife every year, but cycling and travelling seemed to drag me away. I left the Hospital and started at once for Italy, where I spent the winter, and on my return I felt I had been too long out of practice to resume the work.

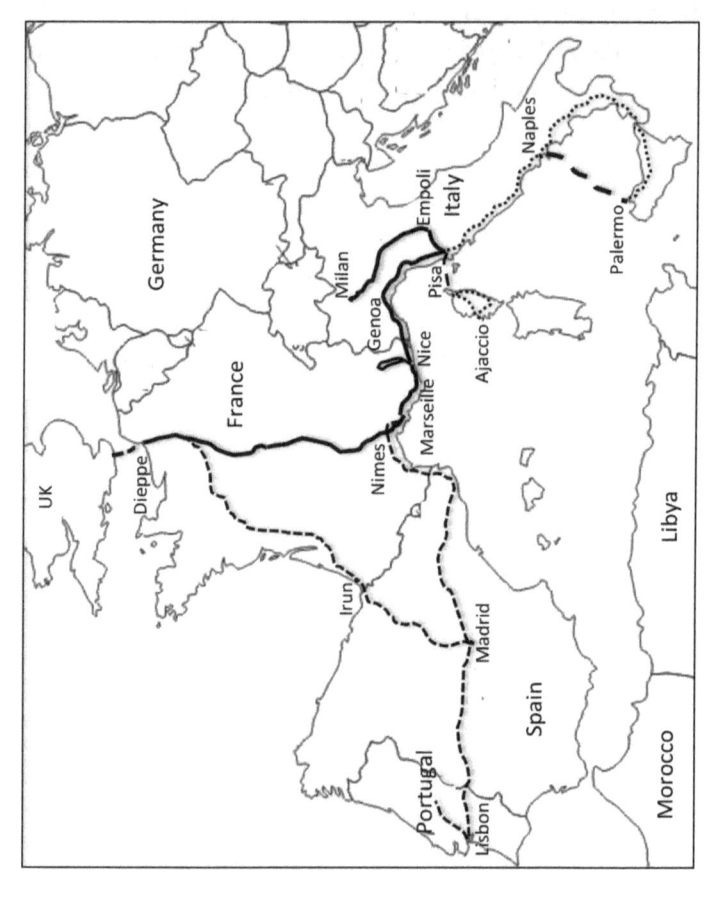

Map 2: Three of many cycle journeys through France, Italy and Spain

CHAPTER X

CYCLING THROUGH ITALY

IN the autumn of 1897 I left England for Italy. Cycling from Dieppe, I reached Naples in the following spring, where I put up at my usual pension. There were two American cyclists staying there at the time. I found that they had done more train work than pedal! They were a Presbyterian minister and his wife, travelling for the sake of their health. Their only child had died, and their parishioners had subscribed £1000 for them to have a good holiday and try to forget their trouble.

I found them delightful companions. Mr. Rogers was descended from one of the pioneers who went out to America in the Mayflower. Fighting for England during the War of Independence, his grandfather lost his land, but in spite of that he stayed in America instead of emigrating to Canada, where land was granted to those who had fought for England.

Mrs. Rogers's ancestors were mostly missionaries. She was a graduate of an American university. Alas! she is dead, and I have lost sight of Mr. Rogers. They became dear friends of mine.

About the end of February 1898 we left together for Sicily. At Naples I had been made an honorary member of the Italian Cycling Club, so on arriving at Palermo I went to see the President of the Sicilian Cycling Club. Meanwhile, Mr. and Mrs. Rogers went to the American Consul, who told them that brigandage was so rife in Sicily that he did not venture even to the Opera without an escort of police. This rather alarmed them, so it looked as if I should have to explore Sicily alone; but during the few days we spent at Palermo, as I met with no unpleasantness whilst going about the neighbourhood alone, they took courage, and we started together. We could not, however, keep together the whole time, as their cycles were not built to stand the bad roads we encountered, so they trained a good deal and we met in the big towns.

A friend of the Rogers's wrote the following lines, I can scarcely call them "verse":

Two modern dames were riding in fair Sicilian land,
When suddenly a brigand man bade them dismount and stand.
"Give me your money sharp," said he, "don't hesitate or scoff
Or with this keen coltello I'll cut your heads right off."

*They with their hat-pins long and sharp this brigand
man did stab
And in the tenderest place they gave him many a jab
Until he loud for mercy cried and fell down at their feet.
Calmly then they rode away and left him in the street.*

Early in March I crossed from Messina to Reggio Calabria – the latter town was devastated by an earthquake shortly after I was there – with the intention of riding through the centre of Calabria.

The President of the Palermo Cycling Club had given me an introduction to the President of the Reggio Club, who arranged for an escort of cyclists to show me round Reggio the morning after my arrival, and they were then to set me on my road. They escorted me along the coast as far as Scilla, and from there I dived into the mountains. The first climb was 1,600ft. to a sizable town, I think called Montelone.

On starting next morning, I found the mounted troops mustering in preparation to go off to the north, I think to Luino on Lago Maggiore, where an insurrection had broken out. When I came along they formed up in two lines, and I had to cycle down between them, they cheering loudly the whole time! I was truly glad to be out of the town and on the quiet road again.

My first adventure was with a country-woman driving a mule laden with a sack of grain, I rang my bell, but the woman did not go to the mule's head, so it played up and kicked off the sack of corn, which burst! I had to be callous and ride off, leaving the woman lamenting. I could do nothing to help, and if I had stayed her yells might have brought her assistance and probably trouble for me. I found the roads fairly good, but of course hilly. The peasants were dressed in picturesque national costume, very different from the rags worn in all the towns and villages south of Naples. It was raining and looked as if the rain would turn to snow, so I rode and walked as fast as I could all that day. I stopped only a short time for refreshment, which I took in the shape of eggs beaten up in wine.

Some of my nights' lodgings were decidedly rough, but always clean. Occasionally I came across a nice hotel when I wanted to stop for the night. One particularly, at Tirrolo, was very nice but crowded with officers on their way north. I was wet and tired. Fortunately one of the officers said he would give his room up to me. A crowd followed me upstairs (all men). I thought I would never get my room to myself. I was longing for a wash, and the small amount of hot water that I had obtained with difficulty was getting cold. The last of my escort to leave the room was the man who had given it up to me. I think he quite thought we were going to share it! I did not venture downstairs again that night, but managed to get some bread and milk brought up to me. Next morning all was quiet, the troops having gone off early.

The next five days were spent alternately riding and walking over hilly ground made more difficult by heavy rain. I spent some time at a small town called Murmanno to get my clothes dried and shoes mended.

I think that some of the men who flocked into the villages, where I stopped for refreshment, must have been brigands. They did not molest me. I could understand them, although I told them I did not speak Italian.

The next place of interest was Cosenza, where Alaric, King of the Visigoths, died after sacking Rome. The legend is that he is buried in a coffin of gold inside one of iron where two streams cross. The funeral took place at night, and the captives who did the work were all put to death so that the secret burial place should not be revealed.

After Cosenza I got as far as Lake Lagonagro, out of the brigand zone. Riding through a village, I noticed many of the inhabitants standing at their doors looking at newspapers and then at me. I found out afterwards that they were reading an account of my riding in Calabria, and I suppose they were interested to see me in the flesh after having come through the brigand country.

My tyres were pretty well worn out. Also I was nearly at the end of my repairing outfit. To make matters worse I was benighted. It was too dark to read the signposts, and I was fairly lost. It was a beautiful night, and I was just beginning to think I must sleep out when I met a man who directed me to a village, where another man directed me to the only house showing a light. On entering, I found the dwellingroom full of men. Upstairs was a large sleeping place, a sort of loft. The men kindly with one accord gave up their accommodation to me. A nice motherly old landlady assured me I would be quite safe, as she slept just outside the door.

I don't know what became of the men, the place was quite quiet at daylight when I arose and tried to mend punctures. I came to the end of patches and solution without success, so had to make my way on foot to the nearest town, Battiphaglia by name; but it boasted of no cycle shop or anywhere to get a repairing outfit. I tried in vain with makeshifts, even with gum and postage stamps! Luckily the town possessed a station and railway, so I trained to Naples and went straight to my old pension. It was only my dilapidated garments and much reduced weight that convinced my friends that I had cycled through the heart of Calabria.

In Sicily some youths, who were minding sheep, were rather unpleasant to me. I found that men were usually quite civil, women not always so; but these youths were decidedly unpleasant! I was trundling my cycle up a long hill when two sheep dogs came to have a sniff at me. Being fond of animals, I coaxed them and gave them some bread. When the owners came up to me they tried to set the dogs on me, but we had become friends, and there was "nothing doing." I was nearly at the top of the hill, so was soon able to out distance them. The dogs tried to follow me, and I had to drive them back to their owners.

No tourists entered Calabria at the time I cycled through, on account of the brigands, but they went by the railway which skirts the coast.

CHAPTER XI

CORSICA AND ITALY, 1898

IN the spring of 1898 I was in Southern Italy, where I had wintered. I took passage in a steamer going from Leghorn to Corsica, landing at Bastia when it was nearly dark. I was greeted by a rotten cabbage being thrown at me, but fortunately it missed its mark.

I was the only passenger to land, but had been told where to find a hotel. The one street seemed quite deserted. I did not see a soul, and wondered where the rotten cabbage could have come from, but I thought it best to walk on and take no notice. The hotel was straight ahead of me, and there I spent a comfortable night. Next morning I made a very early start for Ajaccio. The scenery was lovely, but the road was all uphill. Sweet chestnut trees abounded and grew a good way up the hill. The sweet chestnuts that grow there are very large. The horses are fed on them and keep in as good a condition as if they had been fed on oats.

I stayed at several places en route, and eventually arrived at Corte. There I found a good hotel, the chief room being quite smart with blue chintz. The smartening up had been done in honour of a Mr. and Mrs. Ashmead Bartlett, nee Burdett-Coutts. They had been staying for the sport of wild-sheep shooting. The landlady, on the strength of having entertained them in her extremely modest hotel, considered she was justified in putting up her terms for me, but when I expostulated she was well pleased to accept the ordinary charge, viz. five lire a day.

To Corte I had walked the whole way, as the road was all uphill and steep. Most of the houses I passed on the road to and after leaving Corte had their own little burial places. Vendetta (vengeance), the chief characteristic of the people, reigned supreme even after death. In many cases neighbours could not be buried side by side.

Brigandage did not seem so pronounced as in Calabria, but vengeance had been carried on from generation to generation; little alteration had taken place in that respect since H. Seton Merriman's "The Isle of Unrest" was written, to which book I refer readers for a description of the lovely scenery, too beautiful for my feeble pen to attempt to describe.

I do not remember meeting anyone on the road, and yet in Corsica in those days one never felt alone when in the maquis (bush), as it was full of outlaws who had carried out a vendetta and were escaping justice. These outlaws were secretly supplied with food and information as to where and when the gendarmes were in search of them, and they always seemed to escape justice. They were not brigands, so I was in no danger. It was a weird feeling when in a maquis alone and yet knowing there was someone nearby, watching you. I never wore any jewellery or dressed in a style that could give the impression that I was wealthy. Possibly that often saved me from unpleasant encounters.

The scrub in the maquis consisted mostly of arbutus, the red berries of which looked tempting, somewhat resembling strawberries; but one must be very hungry to eat them, as they are most insipid. Probably the outlaws made use of them.

From the top of the pass it is a long way down to Ajaccio, which I found to be quite a civilised place with a nice hotel, where I rejoiced, unexpectedly, to find a friend, a Miss Rogers, who had been wintering there. I had met her before in out-of-the-way places, and we had often discussed and made plans for going to Tibet together. That was before the days of cycling.

Miss Rogers had not taken to cycling, but was a keen traveller. A musical career was what she was aiming at, but she had the misfortune to break her wrist when skating, just as she was taking her finishing lessons at Leipzig and was hoping to make her debut as a pianist. Her accident put a stop to any idea like that, so she put her musical talent into composition of song accompaniments, but found great difficulty in getting words suited to her music, and when found, still more difficulty in getting her songs sung and known, although many of them were quite pretty. She had small means which enabled her to travel, but I have not met her since our chance meeting at Ajaccio.

There were two keen cyclists living in Ajaccio, who took me for rides in the neighbourhood. I had no companions when walking, but the maquis had an indescribable charm for me, and I wandered about alone, never feeling lonely. There was not much to see in Ajaccio beyond the house where Napoleon was born.

On leaving Ajaccio, I followed the east coast and did not have any particular adventures. There was rather more traffic, and any mules I met seemed very shy of the bicycle. One poor beast was dragging a heavy farm cart, and was so frightened at the sight of my bicycle that he kicked right over the shaft, bringing the cart over too. I was afraid the shaft would choke the mule, but thought it wiser to leave the owner to release him, for my feeble services would have been futile, so rode on, fearing more trouble if I delayed.

I always rang my bell when I wanted to pass animals on the road, but the owners did not always understand and failed to go to their heads in time, so there was trouble sometimes.

I stayed for a few days in a village with a widow who had an only son, a good-looking youth dressed in the usual brown velveteen costume of the country. He generally had a gun in his hand, as shooting was the only work he condescended to do. He was civil to me, but did not offer to clean my bicycle.

The mother, evidently judging from my bicycle, a Singer Grand Modèle de Luxe, thought that I must be a person of means, and set her wits to work to arrange a marriage between her son and I. Although I was old enough to be his mother, that had no weight with her, her one thought being to find him a wife who would keep him in comfort and idleness. When I declined the honour which she thought she was conferring on me, she did not take it amiss and we parted good friends. No vendetta was practised on me. I think the son preferred to keep his powder and shot for filling his mother's larder.

The boat on which I returned from Bastia to Leghorn was crowded with Italian farm labourers returning home after having tilled the land and sewn the crops. Corsicans will not till their own land; they hire Italians to do it for them.

On arriving at Leghorn, I waited on the boat for some time in vain for my bicycle, not wishing to land without it. Previously, when landing at Naples, I had left my bicycle on board, being assured that I would find it at the Customs the next day. I went to the Customs for it the next day and for several next days, and when I eventually obtained it, it was minus tools and pump, and an attempt had even been made to get off the celluloid gear case. I had to send to Coventry for the renewal of the missing articles, and waited at Naples till they arrived. I could not get any redress.

After all, I was obliged to land at Leghorn without my bicycle, but was determined not to leave the Custom

House without it. I made myself as objectionable as I could, hoping they would hurry up and give me my bicycle to get rid of me. I sat in the office and scowled, telling the head of the department that until I had my bicycle I refused to move; he all the time, poor man, was trying to write. At last, exasperated beyond endurance, he ordered a boat to be sent to the steamer to fetch my bicycle. Nothing had been stolen this time. On handing it over to me he said, "You look as if you had regained a lost child!" "I feel like it," I replied, and asked if there was anything to pay. "You can give the man who fetched it a lira if you like," he said, which I gladly did, bade farewell, mounted my bicycle, and was off.

CHAPTER XII

MADEIRA AND SPAIN

AFTER spending the autumn in the Riviera, I made direct for Marseilles and caught a steamer bound for Madeira, as I had promised to winter there with a friend. We shared a "quinta" (a house). My friend was very lame and delicate, and for years she had wintered at Funchal. In those days walking at Funchal was a difficulty. There were no level paths, pebbles were everywhere and there were no roads for cycling. A small stretch of road had been asphalted, but as it had never been repaired since first laid, it was all hills and dales. One had to get a considerable distance out of Funchal before finding a path on which to walk with any comfort. This did not affect my friend, as she could not walk any distance. She hired either a hammock or a bullock cart for her long trips.

My friend was older than myself, the daughter of a clergyman; she had not travelled a great deal, in fact, not much beyond Madeira. She had rather Victorian ideas. She strongly disapproved of my cycling, so her first request on my arrival was that I would not cycle or even talk about it when she introduced me to her friends. I told her that being a member of the Pioneer Club, I felt it incumbent on me that I should endeavour to "ride" over such prejudices. She then begged me not to be in a hurry to ride or talk of riding before she had made enquiries; so off she went to the Mrs. Grundy of the island, from whom she learned that someone in Madeira society had just returned from a trip to England, and had been telling her friends that cycling was becoming quite the rage and fashion. So my friend was quite reconciled. The only spot fit for riding was a very large lawn belonging to our "quinta." My bicycle became a great feature of attraction when we gave afternoon parties in return for the hospitality of our friends. The guests begged me to ride round the lawn, and shouted, "Do it again. Oh! do do it again!"

When we went to lunch at houses of old residents, real old Madeira wine was served. I wonder if there is any to be had now, as the original old vines have long ago died out and have been replaced by an American vine from which is produced a wine of a totally different character. The merchants Cossart & Gordon manufactured a wine with something of a similar taste, but it was far from being like the real old Madeira.

My friend and I had much in common, and by introducing me to all her friends we went out into society a great deal. She always went in her hammock, and I walked by her side, when paying visits. This was not sufficient exercise for me, and she was afraid that I would be wandering off by myself into the hills, so she introduced me to the best walker in the island, who was also noted for her eccentricities. This lady was a German by birth, and had become a naturalised Englishwoman. She had owned a school in Manchester, where the teaching was far in advance of schools of those days. She was the first to introduce Swedish drill.

She was a highly intellectual woman, had very advanced ideas, and, but for her eccentricities, would have been an ideal travelling companion. She lived almost entirely on fruit, uncooked, as she maintained that cooking took away all life-giving properties. Her favourite motto was, "To the pure all things are pure," but those sentiments led her to bathe or take sun-baths whenever and wherever the fancy took her. She was the only pedestrian my friend could think of to serve as a walking companion for me. She was not happy unless she did her twenty miles a day. On account of her fruit-eating propensities we nicknamed her "Pomona." "Pomona" was about the same age as myself, and my walking powers appealed to her. I think that was the reason why she followed me about.

After I left Madeira I met her at Rome, Naples, Capri, Syracuse, and other places. She was quite good company – better than a guide or Baedeker but her eccentricities led her to such peculiarities that I always avoided staying in the same hotel with her.

My friend did not like or approve of "Pomona," but it was a case of walking with her or alone. "Pomona" was delighted to have a companion, and we arranged for a few days' walking tour in Madeira. Walking was very good in the hills and the scenery beautiful. "Pomona" could only carry in her small swag enough fruit for one meal. The first evening where we put up we were beyond the fruit growing zone, so poor "Pomona" had difficulty in ordering her meal, which had to be of vegetables.

She had fixed ideas regarding the arrangement of the furniture in her bedroom. She insisted that she must have her back to the light, so on this occasion at least all the furniture had to be shifted. These trifles were not likely to put her on good terms with her landlord or landlady, and decided me never to travel with her, although I thoroughly appreciated the intellectual side of her character. I discovered too that the peasants whom we met seemed to take a dislike to her. They only laughed in her face when she enquired the way, although she spoke Portuguese fluently. The cause of this, I heard later from my friend's Portuguese maid, was on account of her red hair, and because she went about the hills without a hat, bathed wherever the fancy took her, and did sundry other things which made them think she was mad.

Later, she came to England and bought a Singer Modèle de Luxe, intending to cycle with me, but that never came off. Hers was a man's machine, and she cycled in knickers[6]. For years she spent her winters in Rome, and summers at

---

6. Cycling bloomers

Sanary près Toulon. We met at times and corresponded up to the time of the Great War. Directly the war was over, I cycled again in Germany and France. When in France I went to Sanary to get news of "Pomona." I was told some most extraordinary stories of what had happened to her during the war, which I found to be untrue.

I came across two ladies who had really been intimate with her, and they told me that she had been suspected of being a spy, but as she was a naturalised Englishwoman, she escaped imprisonment. She had died during the war on the island of Ischia, where she was buried. Poor "Pomona," she really was too much in advance of her time. I learned a great deal from "Pomona" during our few days' walking tour, of physiology and other -ologies, and she was well informed in French literature, all of which I fully appreciated, but I felt she had no affection for me. She simply sought me because she wanted a walking companion. After I left Madeira she was attacked and nearly murdered by a peasant when out walking alone in the mountains. The peasant was identified and duly punished.

On leaving Madeira, I went to Lisbon and cycled a little in the neighbourhood. I visited Cintra, now much altered, and from Lisbon I took the train to Madrid.

Cycles were then unknown in Spain and Portugal. At times I met with unpleasant experiences. Stones were often thrown at me, but on those occasions there was generally someone to take my part and send the youthful stonethrower flying. I often saw King Alfonso, then a very small boy, usually driving with his mother, then Regent. He always fixed his eyes with a longing look on my bicycle. I felt sure he would have liked to finger it.

One morning I started out to ride to the Escurial. I passed a church in Madrid where the exhumation of the body of a saint, which had been buried 500 years, was taking place. The body was to be carried in a procession by way of intercession for rain, for there had been a long drought.

Most of the thirty miles to the Escurial I had to do on foot and over a bad road. I saw what appeared in the distance to be villages, but were in fact only ruins. At last I did come to a village and work-people making a road to it. They all left their work and followed me to an inn, where I had some wine, and on leaving they flocked out after me and offered me their wine bottles, out of which they expected me to drink, as they did themselves, from the mouth! I accepted the offer in the spirit in which it was intended. They had never seen a bicycle and were much interested.

As it took me all day getting to and going over the Escurial, I went back by train. On arriving in Madrid, I found it was pouring with rain presumably the priests had weather glasses! At Madrid I was a paying guest in a house kept by a German, where German ladies were boarding, and earning their living by acting as duennas to Spanish girls.

They kindly explained their duties to me. Spanish mamas were too fat and too lazy to chaperone their daughters, so they hired duennas for the purpose, who had to exercise much discretion as to whom of the gentlemen admirers who followed them out walking they should encourage. The duenna's duty was to find out whether the follower was desirable, and if so, encourage him until a stage of the courtship was arrived at when he would play the guitar under the window of the room of the girl he was enamoured of. All those old customs have probably died out years ago. Some Spanish girls came with their duennas to the house where I was staying, and I was glad to make their acquaintance.

Of course I went to a bull-fight and managed to sit out the horrible sight.

From Madrid I trained to Irun, the frontier for France, where I was to have had the sum of money returned I had paid on deposit on entering Spain with my bicycle. I did not get it, and felt it was of no use waiting at Irun for it. So I mounted my bicycle and rode through France and so home again.

Map 3: Cycling through Scandinavia

CHAPTER XIII

VISITING SCANDINAVIA

EARLY one autumn I was seized with a desire to visit Scandinavia. As soon as my simple arrangements were made, I crossed to Hamburg with my bicycle. I did not stay there, but cycled out of the town almost immediately to Hagenbeck's Zoo. It seemed to me to be the most wonderful collection of wild animals I had ever seen, and the way they were trained was even more wonderful. Hagenbeck, in those days, supplied performing animals for circuses. I saw performances of elephants, seals, and other animals far surpassing anything of the kind I had ever seen. But what surpassed all was the way young children sat happily in the same large cages with young lions and tigers and played together.

The next place of interest was Wilhelmshaven and the Kiel Canal, then recently completed. The roads were good through Schleswig-Holstein, quite Germanised. In Copenhagen I found that many people understood and spoke German. As I only intended to be a very short time away from England, I did not "do" all the places I passed through thoroughly. In Copenhagen I visited the Royal Pottery Works. The people in the town seemed pleasant and nice, and I left Denmark hoping and intending to return and pay a longer visit.

In Sweden everything seemed so different: country, people, language. Before putting foot on Swedish soil I managed to pick up a few words of the language from a German. I also enquired how far the hotel where I wanted to stay for the night was. The Swedish mile is quite different to ours (seven of our miles equals one Swedish), so the journey was much longer than I thought, and I arrived after dark at the hotel. Fortunately for me there was a German staying there, and he made arrangements about my room and had some of my money changed.

After an early breakfast, I set off on the road again. Passing a private house, I saw the owners having coffee. Longing for a cup myself, I managed to make them understand, and I paid for it by holding out my hand containing small coins for them to take what they pleased. I was much fortified with the coffee, but towards midday began to feel famished. I saw no signs of life anywhere – everlasting black pine trees and lakes. At last, at a turning in the main road, I beheld a very tumbled-down signpost, on which with difficulty I made out a word that had some resemblance to the German word "Hülfsstätte" so I followed the sign and found a really nice restaurant.

I aired one of the few Swedish sentences I had acquired, implying that I wanted something to eat. I thought the waitress did not understand me, and of course I did not understand her. A couple at a table were enjoying a good hot meal. I pointed to what they were eating, and still we could not understand each other. I went up to and pointed to some eggs – still no result – so I made for the door. The attendant followed me. I turned round and asked her for milk and bread, which words I had learned. These she brought me, for which I was grateful. She would not take any payment. Milk was very, very cheap in Sweden; that probably accounts for her not charging me.

Before requiring another meal, I became acquainted with some of the customs and habits of the country, one of which was, and is still, I believe, that you help yourself at a restaurant from a selection of hors d'oeuvre on a sideboard, for which no charge is made, before ordering something from the menu.

The everlasting black trees and lakes seemed to have a depressing effect on one. I was told that Sweden was noted for the many suicides that take place there.

I came across some Germans working in the forest, and with their help and the bit of Swedish I had mastered I encountered no more difficulties on the road. I was making for Stockholm, and, when within about two days' ride, I passed through a village where I met two ladies, one of whom spoke French. She advised me to stay at the little hotel in the village, which was cheap and comfortable. Having already ridden seventy miles that day, I decided to remain. The lady kindly acted "spokesman" with the landlady of the hotel. My bill for supper, bed, and breakfast came to one shilling of our money. Certainly my supper consisted only of bread and milk!

While rubbing up my bicycle, my new acquaintance told me she was a doctor taking her holiday. She held an appointment at the principal hospital in Stockholm. She gave me her address, also that of a hotel where she recommended me to stay. She told me that she was returning to Stockholm the next day, and that if I telephoned to her on my arrival she would devote all the time she could spare to showing me the sights of the city.

On arriving at Stockholm, I telephoned as arranged, and the lady doctor carried out her promise to act as guide, and she certainly made the most of the short time I had at my disposal. On looking back I realise what an interesting town Stockholm is. I am afraid I did not make the best of my time there, neither did I pick the brains of the lady doctor sufficiently! I was greatly interested just then in hospitals and infirmaries. I had recently been learning to dispense at a large infirmary of which a nephew of mine was chief medical officer.

The lady doctor met me and asked me what I would like to see. I expressed a wish to go over her hospital, also an infirmary. She arranged for other members of the staff to accompany us round. It was curious to hear the number of different languages that were spoken amongst us. The chief medical officer in lunacy was a German. I was able to converse with him and in French with the lady doctor. From the hospital we went to the infirmary, and there I saw many things that if adopted in England would be an improvement, especially that the old and infirm married couples were not in separate wards.

I was greatly interested in the zoological gardens. It seemed more like an outdoor museum than a zoo. An encampment of Eskimos and their dogs and reindeer appealed greatly to me.

I left Stockholm with regret and started off again on my bicycle. At Carlstad I tried to get a map of Norway, but there was not one to be had. Norway had recently separated from Sweden, and the Swedes were still very sore on the subject. As I was unable to get a map, I was obliged to find my way to Bergen by asking. The Norwegians are a friendly people, and many could speak a little English. I was even offered hospitality, which I would gladly have accepted, but I felt that my cycling dress was too shabby.

The country through which I rode was hilly and beautiful. Having no map, I did not know the names of the places I passed through. One day I found myself in a lovely valley and in front of me was a high cliff, and from my point of vantage I could not see where it was possible for a road to be. On arriving at the foot of the cliff, I found that a very narrow road zigzagged all the way up to the top. At intervals of about every fifty yards there was a resting place. A man kindly offered to trundle my bicycle up for me, but he gave up after the first stage. By taking things slowly and resting often, I at last arrived at the top. Tiny carts drawn by tiny ponies were going up the hill.

At Bergen I found quite nice company at the hotel where I stayed. Everyone spoke so well of our Princess married to the then Crown Prince; they admired her so much for her simple way of living. They told me that when she went out shopping she carried her purchases home just as they did. That pleased them immensely. As for her little son, now the Crown Prince, the ladies said they loved him so much they felt they could eat him!!

From Bergen I crossed by steamer to Hull and cycled home to Ealing. With the exception of the Swedish lady doctor, I must own that I prefer the Norwegians.

CHAPTER XIV

CYCLING IN EASTERN EUROPE, 1904

HAVING explored most of Southern and Western Europe, I decided in the autumn of 1904 to see something of Eastern Europe, and to make for the Polands, partly to find out for myself if any feeling of nationality still remained after years of misrule by Germany, Russia, and Austria.

August 25th found me on the road to Parkeston Quay[7]. I arrived at Hamburg at 5.30 the next morning, where I refreshed myself at a good cafe and enquired how to get out of Hamburg to Mecklenburg. As I had been very sea-sick, I did not enjoy the six miles of cobbles I was obliged to cover. The cobbles passed, I found the roads splendid, and as I had a favourable wind there was no

---

7. The old name for Harwich, Essex.

difficulty in covering the ground at a good pace, except for the cobbles in every town and village.

As my destination was Warsaw, I will not dwell on the little detour in the Mecklenburg "Switzerland" beyond saying that it is a charming place for a cycling tour for those who do not object to hill climbing. The beauties consist chiefly of pretty little lakes, plenty of varied timber, and villages picturesquely situated, throwing their reflection on the water of the lakes. At Schwerin, I was given correct information by the owner of a cycle shop as to the best roads on my map to follow to Posen.

The evening of the second day I arrived at a suburb of Berlin, 196 miles from Hamburg. To get through Berlin I again enquired from the owner of a cycle shop, who kindly wrote down the names of streets and sketched a little plan, by following which the riding was mostly on asphalt. There had been no rain for four months in and around Berlin, and that was probably the cause of twenty miles of bad roads. In the country, "Sedan" celebrations were taking place – all the inhabitants of the villages were going to the most popular beer-gardens, where they met friends and drank together and listened to a band.

One Sunday I had to stay the night at a little country hotel where there was a ball going on. I was too tired to stop up to witness it, but I might just as well have done so as to have tried to sleep. The band played lively dance music nearly the whole night. German dancing is very quick and energetic.

On starting next morning, I found much broken crockery had to be avoided in the road on account of a "Polterabend" having taken place. In Northern Germany on the eve of a marriage every friend and acquaintance of the bride who wishes her well brings a bit of crockery and throws it at her door.

With good roads and a still favourable wind, Prussian Poland was soon reached. Miles of forest marked the frontier. Emerging from the forest, the extreme poverty of the peasants impressed me with the fact that I was out of Germany proper. Women went bare-foot and worked like men or even harder. I saw instances of women carrying and dragging loads while idle men stood by or walked at their side, a sure sign of a low state of civilisation.

The Fatherland was doing its best to Germanise and civilise that part of Poland, but the inhabitants were not appreciating the methods used, at the time of my visit, so the process was a slow one. Food, with the exception of sausages in great variety and bread, milk and eggs, was difficult to obtain. Sausages began to pall on me, and I was longing to have a really good dinner once more, so I timed my arrival at Posen for about noon, the dinner hour at every restaurant. But I was terribly disappointed to find that no dinners were served unless previously ordered.

In despair and disgust I left Posen dinnerless and took a short cut without observing a notice to the effect that I was in a prohibited area. I was soon stopped by a policeman. I told him I had been directed that way and was sorry if I was trespassing, but that I would go back

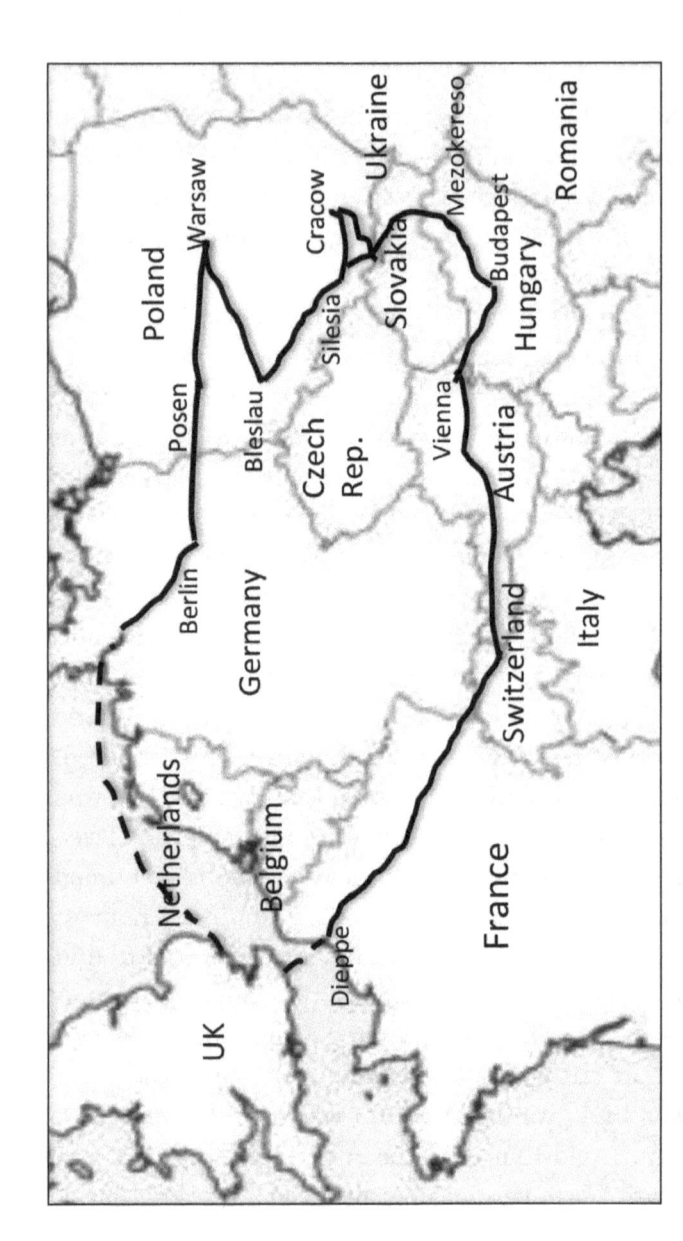

Map 4: Bicycle journey through Eastern Europe

Note: Austrian Hungarian empire included Czech Rep. and Slovakia in 1918. Russia included much of Poland and all Ukraine.

if he wished. Whereupon he permitted me to pass, and directed me to another restaurant. I was by this time quite famished and prepared for even cold sausage, when a kind old gentleman, having heard my pitiful appeal for at least some soup, retired in my favour, i.e. gave up his dinner to me, but after all it was only soup, hot sausage, and brown bread. But I was grateful even for that.

Soon I reached the Russian frontier, and I saw great changes in the people, roads, food, and drinks. In the last German village I was in I realised that I was in the land where the Russian poultry we hear so much about comes from. The village was full of geese that had just crossed the frontier. Carts were piled with crates filled to suffocation with chickens. Here, too, I saw the first specimen of the Jew with whose appearance I was to become familiar, the type my readers may have seen in Whitechapel and Stepney. This great poultry trade was in the hands of the Jews.

The following morning my troubles began. My intention was to ride to Warsaw, and from there on to Cracow. A Jewess, acting as interpreter, kindly explained my plans to the Custom House officer. He charged me twenty-seven roubles, assuring me that the sum would be repaid at any frontier Custom House by which I left Russia for Austrian Poland. He took a very minute description of my bicycle, especially of the handlebars, which contained the pump.

He was looking for contraband goods, which he would have found in the string bag hanging on the handlebar in the form of English newspapers with the latest accounts of Russian defeats by the Japanese. Russia and Japan were then at war and the inhabitants of Russian Poland were absolutely ignorant as to what was taking place and thought they were on the winning side all the time. He was very undecided as to the name of the makers of my bicycle. He did not know whether to select "Special", "Coventry", or "Singer" as the maker's name. I pointed to "Singer." "Oh yes" he said, "sewing machine man" and performed the action of turning a handle. "No, not the same," I replied, "but never mind, hurry up." Finally he tried to bow me out of the office without either stamping the machine or giving a formal receipt for the twenty-seven roubles. I declined to leave without an acknowledgment for the money I had paid, but had to depart eventually with an informal receipt.

Once over the frontier, I realised I had paid dearly to ride on an execrable road. For about a mile I met flocks of geese attended by a cart to pick up weaklings. There were also carts packed high with crates of fowls.

The Jews in Russia came originally from Germany, having been expelled from there, and they have kept their native tongue. They had, with all their apparent poverty, schools for their children. With their natural shrewdness and a little education, it is not surprising they got the better of the poor ignorant Russian peasant. If I had to make an enquiry or seek information, it was always a Jew who came to my assistance, so, metaphorically speaking, "I was in the hands of the Jews."

At length I entered Warsaw by the most horrible suburbs – five miles of roughly cobbled road, with a filthy ditch on each side spanned at intervals by rotten wooden bridges. I was obliged to walk, cycling being impossible. When walking, I was followed by boys and yelping dogs, which I outdistanced when I could ride, but as soon as I dismounted they collected about me again. At last I reached a fairly well paved street, where I found a respectable looking shop, which I entered and enquired for a good hotel. It was growing dark. I followed the directions given, and found myself where I least wanted to be, viz. amongst Jews, but fortunately in the respectable Jewish quarter of Warsaw.

I engaged a comfortable room. No sooner had I taken my room than my passport was demanded. A great deal of formality was expended on it. It was, however, returned to me when I was leaving. I must own to feeling uneasy whilst it was out of my possession, and was glad when it was returned with a permit to leave Russia. The Government put every obstacle in the way of those entering or leaving the country.

The time not spent in officialdom, in connection with my passport and bicycle, I used in seeing the sights. A Polish lady, a chance acquaintance, showed me great kindness and hospitality and took me to see all there was of interest. There were a few beautiful Greek churches (Byzantine style), a new art gallery containing some quite modern pictures, and there was also a fashionable drive and some well-laid-out gardens.

In the art gallery was a striking picture of the last hereditary King of Poland at the deathbed of his wife. She had been poisoned by his mother to make way for a more ambitious marriage for him. He never married again, and on his death, Poland's internal troubles began, leading to Russia, Austria, and Prussia dividing the country between them.

One day we went to see the Vistula, then very low, owing to the long drought. Cossack and Russian soldiers were stationed there to overawe the inhabitants, for the detested Government feared that advantage might be taken of the war then going on, to create disturbances. What chance had the poor things of causing any trouble, for all their young men had been drafted to the front and the age for conscription lowered to eighteen from twenty-one?

When I wanted to leave Warsaw I had some difficulty. I had by that time discovered that the receipt given me at the frontier was, as I thought it to be, valueless; but I obtained with the help of the English Consul a letter to the head of the Customs at Warsaw, who was to send it on to his colleague in Shipca. This letter was intended to bring dire punishment on the underling who, through ignorance or dishonesty, had failed in his duty and given me a worthless receipt. The result was I received my twenty-seven roubles back, and I think it was a lesson to the Russian officials to respect the holder of an English passport.

I cannot recommend Russian hotels either for comfort or cleanliness, and those kept by Poles and Slavs in Prussian Poland were certainly no better. In Russian

Poland, there was a great falling off in the breed of horses and cattle. Probably most of the good horses had been drafted to the war.

The dogs were a great nuisance. One upset me, but I forgave him, as he only got in front of my bicycle to obey his master's orders to clear the road for me through a herd of cattle. Another dog seized and tore my skirt. The road being too rough for me to escape by flight from the dogs, I had continually to dismount and defend myself with stones and sticks.

The peasant women no longer went barefooted like the Prussian Polish women, but wore high boots like men and short skirts. I was glad to follow their fashion in dress, it rendered me less conspicuous, and I was sorry when the time came to resume my long dress. I was obliged to leave by the same frontier by which I had entered, but not relishing the unpleasantness of the suburbs of Warsaw again, I trained as far as there was a line, which was nearly half the way to the frontier. The country was pretty, and there were many hamlets dotted about which looked tranquil and pleasant when the dirt and poverty of the interiors were beyond sight.

In the country, the peasants seemed to take their Sunday recreation in making their overworked horses drag them about in long springless carts lined with basketwork, the whole crowd sitting on the floor of the cart as tightly as they could squeeze. On the Sunday I saw them, it was towards the evening and the roads were quite gay with these parties. The horses frequently shied at my bicycle. The pleasure seekers and I laughed and chaffed together, of course not in the least understanding each other. We pulled up together at a wayside refreshment place and took Russian tea and parted the best of friends.

I was not sorry to leave Warsaw. A veil of sadness seemed to hang over the place. A feeling of happiness came over me when I crossed the frontier and, owing to the letter I have referred to, received prompt attention and civility. I was glad to find myself back in Prussian Poland and under the protection of the Fatherland. Everything was cleaner. The women wore clean white caps which gave them quite a French look. Until well into Silesia, difficulties beset me in the country districts. It was not always easy to get accommodation at night before darkness set in.

I was hugging the Russian frontier and had taken the main road to Breslau. I found the people suspicious of strangers. Silesia is civilised and Germanised to the extent of having smoky towns. My last bit of rustic Poland ended with a beautiful pine forest, where I was struck with the number of birds and butterflies, especially the "Camberwell Beauty," then nearly extinct in England; but it had the usual Continental yellow rims to its wings instead of white, as in England.

After leaving the forest, I entered the coal district and passed through ten miles of dirty, smoky, and cobbled towns connected by tramlines, which only ended shortly before reaching the Galician frontier, where the country became pretty, but very hilly.

At the last German frontier town I had come to the end of my maps, and was counting on getting a fresh supply to take me through Galicia and Hungary, but none were to be had, and I was sent to a banker as being the most likely man to give me information about the road to Cracow. He changed money for me, but his directions proved utterly wrong. He strongly advised me to train to the first town, about thirteen kilometres distant, saying that for some way after crossing the frontier there was no road. It was a glorious evening, and walking to me was preferable to the train.

His directions brought me to the frontier, but the road was only for foot passengers, not even bicycles! I was sent round what seemed to me miles, over a sandy waste, to cross over the frontier at the right place, which was of course by the main road. Between a bridge that I crossed and the actual frontier was a large space, a sort of no man's land of which the roughest and wildest of Jews had taken possession. I had a warm reception, and found it better to face the rabble on foot, so as to protect my bicycle from molestation. The boys had sticks in their hands and mischief in their eyes! Those sticks were aimed at my spokes, but I ran the gauntlet and came through unscathed.

I reached the Custom House close to the frontier and was not delayed there long. An official told me of a town nine miles distant where there was a good hotel, so I mounted and was soon on a lovely running track through a pine forest. What a relief to be quiet after my adventures with the unruly boys and the unpleasantness of the smoky towns! I enjoyed the perfect solitude of the forest for some miles.

Just outside the forest was a small village inhabited entirely by Slavs. There were no Jews, so my knowledge of German did not help me. I tried to verify my road and showed the little list of towns the banker had given me to one of the villagers, but could not arrive at anything definite except that something was wrong, so I thought the best thing to do was to ride on in faith, trusting to what the Austrian official had told me.

At last I found the town he mentioned. At first sight I was not impressed, probably because I entered it through the low Jewish quarter. I noticed the Galician Jew seemed much lighter hearted and frolicsome than the Russian Jews. The town improved as I rode on, and at length I saw a respectable looking man, so asked him to direct me to a hotel. Evidently his directions were not very accurate, for I rode backwards and forwards for some time before I spotted the hotel. It was stowed away in such a funny little street and had no sign. I had not learned the Slav for "inn" but I took care to do so that night. It was a comfortable hotel, with plenty of agreeable company in the public room, and I spent a pleasant evening gathering information about the neighbourhood and also directions as how to get to Cracow.

I was now riding parallel to the Carpathians, and the country was magnificent. The ruins of castles that I saw from time to time enabled me to realise that Poland had a history! The road was very bumpy and bad, but I was getting used to that sort of treatment. In Russia the roads were metalled but hard and only out of repair but here in Poland they had never been well made. Great boulders were left in the road, and paths worn over, round or between them which my machine literally bounded over. I realised that I was in the land of bears and wolves, but fortunately I did not come across any.

Cracow is only a very small town. A few hours of its noise and racket was enough to inspire me with no wish to stay. I bought some new maps, collected my letters from the post office, close to which I found a restaurant, where I refreshed myself and answered what letters required attention, and was off again as soon as possible to the Carpathians, intending to put up at a village about ten miles distant. By the time I had finished my letters it had begun to rain, so I decided to stay the night in Cracow after all. But fate decided otherwise. The inn I selected was large, but did not look inviting. The landlady, hearing I intended to stay till the next morning, emphatically said "No" and turned her back on me. I pleaded fatigue and the state of the weather, but she remained adamant. Her young son evidently thought it rough on me and followed me out to explain that it was Friday, the eve of their Sabbath, and their religion prevented them taking payment on that day. I felt too indignant to return. I would have paid her overnight, and all would have been well if only she had explained matters at the beginning.

Night was coming on. How I managed to ride nearly ten miles in the dark I do not know. I did not see or hear any bears or wolves, but there were some big creatures flopping in the trees, eagles I presume. I had the road quite to myself, which was perhaps just as well under the circumstances. I was dead tired when I reached the village, which was in pitch darkness. I met a watchman, and he took me to a large old-fashioned hotel. His knock was answered by a nice little girl of about twelve years of age, who appeared to be the only inmate. She led me to a large room containing several beds. There was nothing to eat in the house, not even milk, but the little girl was able to bring me a bottle of light wine which was excellent and a bit of broken bread. I was really too tired to eat, so I selected my bed and thought I made the girl understand I had hired the whole room.

I made a tour of inspection before retiring for the night. I found double windows which did not open and iron bars in front of them; there were also double doors, but no locks or bolts, so I got into bed and fell asleep. But I was soon awakened by the opening of the door. A woman with a dim candle and two men appeared. I yelled out aghast. They were apparently equally surprised, and quickly shut the door and left me. I barricaded those doors with all the furniture I could move and went to bed again and slept till morning. The intruders had not really frightened me. I realised at once that the little girl had gone to bed without telling her parents that she had let the room. Next morning I had some good coffee for my breakfast.

I had heard so much about the lovely scenery that I began to wonder when I should come across it. I left the main road to go up the Tatra Valley (a much-vaunted place), and reached a health resort, called Jakopane, high up in the mountains, so high up that the mountains below looked stunted. I imagine it was a lovely place in fine weather. Unfortunately, the weather did not favour me whilst I was there. A Polish lady who took in paying guests put me up. She was well informed and interesting – we conversed in French. She played the piano well, and treated me to Polish national airs, prohibited in Russia and German Poland. She also smoked. The pleasant evening was rather marred by the old mother, whose idle curiosity about myself was most annoying.

I was now high up in the Carpathians, and the next day saw me in Hungary. As I had really gone to Poland to satisfy myself about the government of the three Polands, I will give my impressions. If the German Emperor had visited his territory incognito with ears and eyes open, he would have heard enough treason to make his hair stand on end. The German Poles longed to be treated as a free people, and not to have all nationality stamped out; also to become owners of the land. Of course, Russian Poland was unspeakable.

In Galicia one heard no complaints. I was told that all subjects could gain access to the Emperor of Austria, and that he devoted part of every morning to seeing anyone who asked for an audience, and gave preference to the most lowly. The Emperor asked some peasants how they were getting on in Galicia, and the reply was "that they had a plague of white field mice"! These peasants had walked all the way from Galicia to see the Emperor.

In Galicia the Jews are said to hold to their old fashions and customs more than in other countries. One meets men and boys with their funny corkscrew curls hanging over their temples. They also wear long frock-coats. The married women wear wigs, the idea being that when a Jewess is married it is no longer necessary to try to be captivating. The unmarried Jewesses wore their hair fuzzed and dressed out. Many old women wore greasy black silk where their front hair should have been.

The following day I went farther up the Tatra Valley to see another health resort of which I had heard great things. Unfortunately, the weather was bad, but nevertheless I went over the Tatra district, which is in Hungary, and up and down several passes undeniably pretty; but I was rather disappointed after all I had heard in their favour.

In the Jakopane Valley, which is in Galicia, the peasants wear sheep-skin jackets, sometimes the wool outside, sometimes reversed; then the leather is embroidered in bright colours. These jackets give the men a brigandish appearance.

My last day in Galicia was a Sunday made memorable by the number of tipsy men I had to pass on a narrow road; they were sometimes walking three abreast, reeling from side to side. I am glad to say they kept their heads so low they did not see me, so I was able to dodge past them. My midday meal that day I procured at a village inn kept by a Jew. It consisted of what seemed to be curd highly flavoured with spices made up into a heavy paste. I had some good coffee and milk to wash it down.

I crossed into Hungary in time to see how Hungarians spent Sunday. I saw no drunkenness there. In the first village I came to the inhabitants were coming out of church from afternoon service. The women were wearing high boots similar to those I had seen in Russian Poland and short petticoats. It seemed a sensible dress, particularly as all the roads were inches in mire from the recent rain.

In Hungary gipsies were much in evidence – they were a low, bad-looking type. I was assured they would not molest a lonely woman, but probably would not scruple to attack and rob a man. The few men I met on cycles carried pistols. They usually offered to escort me, but I preferred riding alone.

The mountain roads were fairly good, and I had several glorious days in the Carpathians, winding through the valleys. A high head wind caused me to stop early one afternoon, before having accomplished my usual distance of 60 to 100 miles, at a small town, Mezokoreso by name. I was much attracted by the picturesque national costumes of the inhabitants, for it was a fete day, and there was a great display of rich colours and embroideries.

I put up at a comfortable hotel. The landlord, who had been in America, was pleased to have the opportunity of talking English. After a good rest and dinner, the first good one I had had since I left Warsaw, he asked me if I would care to see the national dances which were to be rehearsed for the Vintage Ball. The ballroom was large, but badly lighted. The landlord explained that the band, and all Hungarian bands in fact, are made up of gipsies of the more respectable class. He left me in the ballroom, promising to return when the national dances began, so that he might explain them. I joined some chaperones sitting at the farther end of the room. We could only exchange smiles, as we had no language in common.

As the young ladies entered the room they came straight to the chaperones and kissed the hands of each, mine included, before commencing to dance. The landlord kept his word and returned in time to explain the dances, all of which had some connection with the vintage, and are danced in national costume on the occasion of the real ball.

After this long rest I made an early start and, as the wind had died down, was able to cover a considerable amount of ground before it got up again with increased violence and I had to face a dust storm such as I have only seen equalled in Australia. I toiled against it on foot for hours, as no place of shelter could I find. On reaching a village with a respectable inn, I took shelter under the veranda, then occupied by chickens. The inn was full of noisy people, so the veranda was preferable, although all the children of the village crowded round and gaped at me. I took coffee and wine, but could not recover sufficiently to face the terrible wind and dust again, hoping the wind would drop towards the evening and enable me to reach my destination, about eight miles farther on.

Suddenly a cyclist appeared, the first I had seen since entering Hungary. He had not come by my road, so had not faced the storm. He asked the landlady if I was going to Budapest, about eighty miles distant, and offered to escort me. He knew a little German, and the landlady explained that I did not intend to leave till the wind had dropped, and was then only going to the nearest town, so he rode off. The noisy people having left, I decided to stay at the inn for the night.

The next morning I started early, and after about ten miles was overtaken by the cyclist. He was riding a high geared machine, so left me behind when going downhill, but uphill I was able to out distance him. He showed me a pistol he had for dogs, and it seemed as if they must have smelt it, for they left us in peace. Except for stopping to take off my jacket and for him to oil his machine, a process required every few miles by German machines, we went hard for twenty miles, making in all thirty miles for me. We halted for a drink of milk, and then started off again for another fifteen miles. I began to wonder if my escort ever required a meal. We stopped at a town for him to write a post card, then off again.

I felt that the reputation of my country, my machine, and my sex were all at stake, and rode accordingly, but was not sorry when after another ten miles he took me to a restaurant. Before entering, he gave me his card, which now lies before me. I keep it as a curiosity. It is long and narrow and made of rice paper, and has some hieroglyphics on it which I presume stand for his name. During dinner I found one of my cards to give him. It has probably found its way into a museum, for it must have appeared as curious to him as his did to me.

After dinner I thought surely the young man would like a smoke and I could take the opportunity of slipping quietly out of the town. But not a bit of it; he neither drank nor smoked. Budapest was not far off. I had no wish to spend the night there – I preferred the quiet of the country. Nevertheless, we started off together again, but after we had gone a few miles a shower came on, to my great relief, and we sheltered under a tree. I made him understand (he had little German and I no Hungarian) I did not want to go on in the rain, nor to Budapest, so he rode on alone. I picked up a washer under the tree, and farther on a nut off the young man's machine, and I heard next morning at the Octroi that after leaving me he had not gone far before one of his pedals came off.

At the Octroi he had spread the fame of my wonderful machine, that only required oiling about every 500 miles, and that it had been ridden all the way from Hamburg without anything going wrong, and by a woman too! So I was secretly delighted that I had made such an effort for my country, machine, and sex. Of course, rain had to follow such high wind. It poured during the night and till 3 p.m. the next day.

At a little country place just beyond Budapest I found the soles literally worn off my shoes and other repairs necessary. The village cobbler soled and patched while I watched and conversed with him and admired his workmanship. Then I started off, putting those soles to a severe test. The Hungarian roads are not suited to wet weather. I not only walked that afternoon, but the greater part of the next day, and when the roads did dry they were so rough that riding was not a pleasure.

From Vienna I rode back to England by well-known roads and without more adventures worth mentioning, till I arrived at the French frontier. I crossed into France from Switzerland. At the Custom House I noticed the officers in the cafe, but they did not seem to take any notice of me. I had some coffee there, and as soon as I had finished it I mounted my bicycle, and seeing no Custom House officers on the road went slowly on. Thinking all was well, I put on speed up a long hill, which amused some pedestrians, who called, "Comme vous montez la côte!" and well they might do, for a Custom House officer was riding helter-skelter after me.

I won the race, of which I was quite unaware, and at the top of the hill alighted for a short spell. To my astonishment I saw the officer was "after" me. When he came up to me, he insisted on examining the contents of my small luggage holder. I was not well pleased to see the contents spread out on the road, as I had been quite a month from home and things were a bit travel stained. It was the first occasion it had been opened on passing Custom or Octroi Houses. No doubt this official thought I was trying to give him the slip.

CHAPTER XV

CYCLING ROUND THE WORLD, 1910

I BOOKED by the White Star Line to Boston in 1910. Several friends saw me off from Liverpool Street Station. We spent the waiting time scanning my future fellow passengers. We much scandalised a missionary and his wife by jokingly making remarks as to who looked like bridge players. I happened to be in the same carriage with them to Liverpool, and they were hardly civil, but later, on board, we hit it off all right when they discovered I was not quite a bridge fiend and had other interests in life. There were no good bridge players on board, so I did not play.

I met those missionaries later on a steamer going from Suva in the Fiji Islands to Auckland. On that steamer there were some young men, and the good lady missionary considered it her duty to enquire into their spiritual welfare. She found them well acquainted with the Bible. She asked them what denomination they belonged to. They told her they were "Latter-day Saints." The good lady had never heard of such a denomination, and finding out by enquiry that they were Mormons, she would not speak to them again! One of the young Mormons told me himself.

The voyage to Boston was uneventful. I was met by my American friends, the Rogers, and some other friends. The pleasure of meeting them again soon counteracted the unpleasant feeling of having been classed with the "senile" before landing, because I was over sixty years of age. My friends had engaged me a room. It was rather late in the evening, and dinner was over, but a good meal had been kept for me. It consisted of soup, chicken and vegetables, apple tart and cream, for which I was charged one shilling! At nice restaurants meals were always quite as cheap.

As I had been engaged in political work in England, advocating Tariff Reform when canvassing, food prices interested me. The day after my arrival at Boston I noticed that bread was dear and flour was cheap – that probably accounted for the tiny piece of bread given at restaurants. What astonished me most was to find that boots were no dearer than in England, and there were plenty to choose from with square toes and flat heels.

This reminds me of what occurred when I was canvassing on my return home at Ross. I had been to a Liberal meeting, and the speaker told lies about the prices in protected countries, especially with regard to

America; I was able to refute his assertions, having so recently returned from America. I made good use of this first-hand knowledge when canvassing in the slums, and had to face the threat that I should be thrown into the Wye if I repeated such stories.

My American friends showed me the sights of Boston. Mr. and Mrs. Rogers had their bicycles with them, and we rode out to Rhode Island, needless to mention, the place where the Mayflower emigrants landed. On the Sunday we were there, Mr. Rogers wanted to hear all the sermons he could, so he visited as many churches as possible. A friend of his and I went to Mrs. Eddy's beautiful church, and I well remember the gem of a room she had as her sanctum. We also found our way to Harvard University. Being vacation time girls were then in residence, and we had the pleasure of dining with them. Next day the Rogers and I parted company, they for New York and I for Vermont to visit a nephew, with the understanding we should meet again at Niagara, from where we were to bicycle to Bowling Green, Ohio, where they lived.

On leaving Boston, I was cautioned against stopping for early dinner at a town about twenty miles off, as I was told that I should find everything very dear. On arriving there I enquired my way at a private house and was asked in to dine. I found great hospitality in the States. A lone woman on a bicycle was an unusual sight, and everywhere I was assailed with questions, and frequently my answers found their way into the newspapers. In one town, when wishing an interlocutor farewell, he said,

"Mind you keep good." I thought it great impertinence, but I learned afterwards it was only a common saying which meant, "Mind you keep in good health."

Beyond the big towns the roads were usually bad, and it was only possible to ride on a narrow strip at the side. I found Vermont much behind the times. I was making for a place near Rutland, and on the way saw many forsaken farms left to run wild, and had to fight my way through thick undergrowth. One day I was obliged to take shelter from a heavy shower in a farmhouse, and as the rain looked like continuing, I accepted the invitation of the farmer to stay there. I cannot remember how long I stayed, but long enough for the farmer to ask me to marry him, because, so he said, he could not get anyone to keep house for him. He had several nieces, but they all declined to live with him in spite of his threats to disinherit them for refusing.

Every domicile I passed had its telephone and gramophone, and in the settlements there were funny little arrangements for letters, little boxes that the postman on horseback could reach without dismounting. At length I reached my destination. My nephew was living in a benighted place, and I was glad to hear later he had left. The inhabitants well merited the appellation of "Hayseeds."

I then cycled from Vermont to Rochester and Albany. At Rochester I had an introduction, amongst others, to the manager of a firm of optical instrument makers. As that trade was fast passing from England to Germany and America, I was pleased to find that the manager was an Englishman.

At Albany I noticed the mixed styles of architecture. It looked as if those deputed to design the buildings had travelled in Italy and elsewhere, and, not being able to agree, had each introduced a bit of his own fancy.

When I arrived at Niagara, cycling all the way, my friends had not yet come, so I went into a post office to write some cards. The desk being too high for me, I fainted and fell on to the floor, still clutching the pen in one hand and the stamps in the other. When I came round I found myself in a side office, and am thankful to say no one was fussing me, so I soon recovered. I had probably been overriding, and a good rest set me right.

I crossed over to Canada, but did not get beyond Toronto and Hamilton. On my return to Niagara, my friends had arrived, and we visited the Shredded Wheat Factory, where we were given a free luncheon. I then went with my friends to Bowling Green on a visit to their home. On the way we passed through an Indian reserve, but did not see any Indians. We also went by an oilfield. The smell was most unpleasant, and even reached Bowling Green, when the wind set in that direction. From Bowling Green I cycled to Chicago. Of course, when there, I went over the "sheds," and thought I should never get the sound of the squealing of pigs out of my ears or the horrible smell out of my nose.

I was sorry to leave America without seeing Yellowstone Park, but I was too late in the season and the Park had been closed. The grandeur of the scenery of the Rockies is too well known for me to dwell on. I made a stay at Salt Lake City, and from there trained to San Francisco.

I then went to Honolulu and made a short stay there. I am glad to say the mosquitoes were scarce. From there I went on to Fiji and stayed at Suva, where, of course, I had to drink kava. It tasted like soapy water. The mosquitoes thereabouts were of the worst type, truly dreadful.

I then sailed for Auckland. The accommodation on the steamer was dreadful, and I arrived in Auckland feeling very weak and ill, suffering from blood poisoning due to the Suva mosquitoes! But a few days' rest pulled me round. Until I felt myself again, I did not tell any of my relations and friends of my arrival.

When sufficiently recovered, I started out to see an old Canterbury friend, a neighbour when my husband and I lived in New Zealand. She was a child then, and we were very much attached to each other, although she was much my junior. She had married and left a comfortable home to go up to the then uncivilised north to a place called Umawera. I was hoping to hear from her on my arrival in Auckland, but landed sooner than she expected, and there was no letter of instruction as to how to get to her home. So I started off on my bicycle, trusting to find the way by walking and cycling.

I got on fairly well. I passed a few scattered homesteads and found myself on the gum-fields. I saw a few diggers, either leading a lonely life or working in couples, getting a precarious living by digging over the old ground that had been roughly worked when the gum was so plentiful and large fortunes had been made. Between walking and cycling, I managed to get as far north as Wangarei. There I had to give in, as I could not gain any information as to how to reach my friend; in fact, it was impossible to proceed with a bicycle, so I had to return to Auckland without paying the much looked forward to visit. A letter I received from her later was "blistered" with her tears.

After visits to relations and friends resident in Auckland, I followed the Waikato Valley to Rotorua, where I made a stay to see the wonderful geysers. I had a talk with old Sophy, the Maori woman who was instrumental in saving many English lives when the eruptions took place and the beautiful pink terraces were lost. Waimunga was not active while I was there. A terrible tragedy had recently occurred when two Christchurch girls and a guide were killed. The guide who took me round told me how it happened.

The girls were headstrong and foolhardy, and would persist in going too close to the geyser to take a photograph. A sudden eruption of boiling water and stones took place; their bodies and also that of the guide were washed down to the lake in the boiling water, all the flesh was scalded off their arms, their bangles were found on the bare bones. My guide told me that they must all have been killed instantly by the stones before their bodies were swept down the boiling stream to the lake. The poor mother saw the awful accident from a height above the geyser. The guide I was with took our party as near to an active geyser as was safe. Suddenly an eruption occurred and we were enveloped in steam and quite bewildered, but no one was hurt.

The Maoris were quite civilised in Rotorua; Maori men in white flannels were playing tennis with Europeans. From Rotorua I rode on through the King Country, where I saw a great many wild horses. There were also Maori whares, highly decorated with wood carvings, and English dwellings side by side. I reached Lake Taupo and took the boat across the lake and spent the night on the other side with a lady missionary who lived in a Maori "pah." A Maori woman who was returning from a "tangi" (funeral) came in to see her. She was wearing a Maori mat, which I learned they still adorned themselves in for "tangis."

Some small Maori boys got up a "hake" (war dance) for my entertainment. They contorted their faces, lolled out their tongues, all quite in the proper war-dance style, but they were brandishing sticks instead of weapons. Real Maori weapons then, as now, were only to be found in museums. The grownup Maoris got too excited when performing a "hake" with their original war weapons, so their use had to be forbidden for safety's sake.

The next morning the weather seemed very doubtful, and the township I was making for was fifty miles away. There was no accommodation on the road beyond stables and a harness room used as a sleeping apartment by the man in charge. There was no proper road, just a track made by the wheels of a weekly coach. It was rather rash of me, but I started, having been told it was the day for the coach to run, and that if I found it impossible to walk or ride it could pick me and my bicycle up. Between walking and cycling, not much of the latter, I reached the first stables, only to learn that there was no coach that day. In a case like mine, a lone traveller coming along, the man in charge was supposed to give up his bedroom but I did not like the look of the man, so got some tea and something to eat, pocketed half a scone, and set off once more. The man told me I should come to some water where some men were repairing a bridge, and that they would help me across, which they did, and they were the only human beings I saw till I arrived, nearly dead, at the township I had been told of.

To make matters worse, it came on to rain and it was bitterly cold. It was impossible to ride, so I had to walk. Once I stopped and sat down to rest and finish my bit of scone. I also tried to get at some Kaola tablets I had in my bag, but my fingers were too numb to open the bag! I felt if I sat very long I should be unable to get up at all. Relations at home had prophesied that something of the sort would happen to me, so spurred on with the desire to prove their predictions false I pulled myself together and started off once more on foot. I was told before leaving the first stable that there were other stables on the so-called road where the weekly coach horses were changed. I came to a spot where the wheel tracks branched off; fortunately I fixed on the right track, and soon came to the stables. To have stopped there, soaking wet as I was, would have been fatal.

Before it was quite dark I saw in the far distance the lights of what I knew must be the settlement. On reaching it, I made for the biggest light, which proved to be that of the store, just about to be closed. The owner and his assistants seemed quite taken aback by my appearance. As I was nearly dead with fatigue and travel stained and had forgotten to unpin my skirt, no wonder they stared at me.

One of the men kindly relieved me of my bicycle, and I followed him to the accommodation house. I asked the landlady to give me some hot spirits and water, but prohibition prevailed there. She took me to a wretched bedroom, and left me without offering to get me anything or take my wet clothes away to dry. There was no bell or means of summoning anyone. At length I realised that she did not intend to return, so I rolled myself in a very cottony blanket and tried to sleep; but I could not even close my eyes. I ached all over, whether from the long walk or from rheumatism, I could not make out. Very late next morning I succeeded in calling a chambermaid, and she took all my wet garments to dry in a high wind that was raging. When she returned with them, I managed, still aching terribly, to dress and go down for some breakfast, the poorest and most skimpy meal I have ever seen in New Zealand.

As I had been asked to report on the accommodation houses where I stayed by the Travel Bureau in Christchurch, you may be sure I did not give a good report of this one; in fact, such a report that probably lost the woman her licence. Perhaps it was just as well that I did not have anything to eat when I was in such an exhausted condition, but if the landlady had had a spark of humanity in her composition, she would have given me something hot to drink. She probably had her own gin bottle to go to on the sly.

Although aching all over – and I ached for weeks after I left that accommodation house – I started off directly after my miserable breakfast. There were roads of a sort, but soon after I had gone a little way I found my path blocked by a herd of half wild cattle, and a bull was facing me. How I managed to scramble up a bank to a fence and drag my bicycle with me I do not know! I stood near that fence prepared, in a case of emergency, to get over it. The bull only kept on looking. I think the bicycle puzzled him; anyhow, he did not make for me. After a time a cart came along the road and scattered the cattle in every direction.

I was able to start again, and came presently to a cottage, where there were two women at work in the garden. I asked them the way and was invited in and well feasted. They told me the landlady, in whose house I had spent the previous night, was well known to be a brute, and that steps were being taken to deprive her of her licence. They also told me I was coming to a good metal road. I had not seen such a one for a long time. But alas! The metal road turned out to be stones laid down on a track to which no roller had been applied.

The town I was making for was some distance away, and every bone in my body was aching, but I trudged on, trundling my bicycle. I was presently overtaken by a young man driving an American wagon with a spanking pair of horses. He drew up and offered me a lift. In accepting his kind offer, I saw a difficulty about my bicycle, but he said he would manage that. The way he did manage it was for the bicycle to rest on my knee – that and the jolting over the stones caused me agonies, but as it was a lesser evil than walking, I had to grin and bear it!

We pulled up once to watch a "tangi" for a celebrated old chief, who had been dead for some days, and for whom a great many "tangis" had been held. I noticed that the mourners, mostly Maoris, remained at a respectful distance from the coffin. We did not stay long and soon arrived at a sizable town where I was put down at a good hotel. The young driver would not take any remuneration, so I expressed all the gratitude I felt for his kindness, in spite of the agonies I had suffered. The hotel was full and the bathroom much in request. It was the first bathroom I had come across since leaving Auckland. Probably all accommodation houses have them now. I had to wait my turn. The hot bath, when I did get it, certainly gave slight relief to the pain I was suffering. It was some weeks before I thoroughly recovered.

I was making for New Plymouth. I do not remember any stirring incident on the road but one. I was approaching a fair sized town and, when not far distant, saw two men on the road, one with a trap and the other with a horse. They appeared to be having a leave-taking "stirrup cup" (prohibition was in force in the district). When I came up to them I was met with the usual questions, "Where have you come from and where are you going?" and, "How do you manage about money?" I told them I had friends everywhere and was bound for New Plymouth. Probably it was my shabby appearance that caused them to offer me financial assistance. I had brought an alpaca cycling costume with me from England. The skirt was full and rather long. In places the alpaca had entirely worn away from the lining! I assured them I did not require monetary assistance, but thanked them and said I had sufficient money to take me to New Plymouth.

The road was very bad, and the horsemen, having finished their stirrup cup and parted, one soon overtook me and asked if he might accompany me. I told him that I wanted the whole road, so as to be able to pick my way, as it was in such a bad condition, and too, I wanted to be able to ride when possible. But he would keep up with me, still begging to be allowed at least to give me sufficient money to pay my hotel bill at the next town.

I found out from him that we were not going to the same town and that he would have to turn off at a by-road for his home. The stirrup cup he and his friend had indulged in was apparently taking effect, which showed itself in his repeated insistence to help me. I began to fear I should have to take something in order to quiet him. Just then he lagged a bit, so I put on all speed I could on the bad road and reached a crossroad with a signpost on which was inscribed the name of his town. I took the other road, which I knew led to New Plymouth, and reached there without any further adventures. There I made a long stay so as to fully recover from the effects of the long walk after Lake Taupo.

From New Plymouth I cycled on to Wellington, where I crossed by steamer to the South or Middle Island. From Nelson I followed the West Coast up to Hokitika, where I spent Christmas Day. All up that coast I met a great many cyclists (all men); they helped me over water and funny little bridges, and I received great hospitality everywhere. It was very hot and there were many shallow streams to walk through, so I soon adopted the prevailing fashion of bare legs and wore canvas shoes to protect my feet from the stones.

From Hokitika I eventually got to Christchurch, where, and in the neighbourhood, I made a long stay visiting relations and friends. I had always longed to visit the Fiords, so was determined to do so this time.

The roads were fairly good through Canterbury and Otago, and I rode as far as Lake Te Anau. There I left my bicycle, and took the boat across the lake to the Glade House. The landlady at the hotel of Lake Te Anau told me that my shoes would not hold out to walk to the Fiords. I expected to find that the difficulties were much exaggerated, but on this occasion they certainly were not.

I was delayed at the Glade House by a small party who were waiting to be rowed over the River Clinton, so I joined them, and from the farther side of the river the walking began. Every ten miles there were stopping places, little mountain huts, for excursionists to put up in. They were rough, but quite comfortable, and good plain food was to be had. The track was very rough and my shoes suffered consequently, but the guides patched them up when necessary. Worst of all were the burs. They clung to my long skirt, which, even when cycling, was worn in those days, and they caused dire discomfort. Mosquitoes and sandflies tormented us terribly in spite of the various antidotes the tourists applied.

I spent a very comfortable night at the first mountain hut, but being pressed for time, I decided to walk twenty miles a day instead of the usual ten, so started early next morning alone. I regretted the pleasant companionship I was obliged to leave behind.

The walking was rough – there was much water to walk through and rough rocks to climb over. When I reached the River Clinton, I found it had to be crossed in a most unusual and uncomfortable way – I had to sit on a thing like a tea-tray, which was balanced on a wire; there were no edges to hold on to. An old man was manipulating the "tea-tray." It came to a full stop at times, and I saw the roaring river below me. Mosquitoes and sandflies were devouring me, but I could not spare a hand to fight them, as I was clinging on for dear life to the "tea-tray," but the old man deposited me safely at the landing-stage. From there onwards the track was under repair, in preparation for the passengers who were expected to be landed at the Fiords by the *Waikari*, the steamer which once a year went there, and the passengers landed and walked to the Sutherland Falls.

It was the proprietor of the Sutherland Hotel who discovered the Falls, said to be the highest in the world. The Falls were not very full of water when I passed them, and did not look impressive. I arrived, tired, at the Sutherland Hotel, the only one at the Fiords, so I took a few days' rest, just roaming about the neighbourhood, and then started to walk back again. There had been rain since I came up, so there was much more water to walk through.

It was a Sunday when I started alone on the return journey, and there were no guides on the track, so my shoes got no patching that day. The arrangements for crossing the River Clinton had been greatly improved: a wooden box had been converted into a seat, which had sides one could hold on to, but the wire it ran on was slack and sagged most uncomfortably. I was landed safely and walked on in great discomfort with my poor old shoes trodden over at heel and not much shoe left. An escort came to meet me on reaching the Glade Hotel, so I had company for the last few miles of the walk.

I crossed Lake Te Anau, mounted my bicycle, and made for the first township to get new shoes, and then on to Lake Wakatipu. There I was a little disappointed with the scenery, in praise of which I had heard so much; but perhaps it was the bad weather, no companionship, and the new shoes which were hurting me that prevented me from appreciating the scenery.

I made a very short stay at Queenstown on Lake Wakatipu before going back to Canterbury. I passed through a sandy waste entirely taken possession of by rabbits, which were scuttling about in all directions. There were so many of them they seemed unable to get out of my way. Dotted about on the sand were those curious fungi resembling a sheep's back. A good specimen of one is to be seen in the museum in Kew Gardens.

From Christchurch I went on to Lyttelton, where I took the steamer and crossed to Melbourne. Before leaving England I had been given an introduction to a Mr. and Mrs. Nicolls, said to be the greatest cyclists in Australia. But, alas! I found their cycling days were over. Their home was at Sandringham, about eighty miles from Melbourne, and they had come up to Melbourne to consult doctors. Mr. Nicolls was suffering from creeping paralysis. They were ruralising in the bush a few miles from Melbourne.

Mrs. Nicolls met me on my arrival and took me out to stay with them. They were living in tents and there was a small cottage close by where they took shelter when wet. Mr. Nicolls had a hammock slung in the bush, and there he lay all day, which was mostly passed in playing bridge. We were just a party of four – Mr. and Mrs. Nicolls, a young friend of hers (whose tent I shared), and myself. It was a lovely life, but overshadowed by sadness, as we all knew that Mr. Nicolls could not recover.

After a few days' stay there, Mrs. Nicolls and I started off on our bicycles to her home at Sandringham, which she intended to sell, as there was now no hope of her husband returning to it. When we arrived, dusty and tired, we found everything prepared for us. Friends had tidied up the house, made our beds, and had a good supper ready.

On the way we stopped to have a little rest near Ballarat, called Dead Man's Gully on account of the murders that were committed there when the Ballarat diggings were at the height of their prosperity. Mrs. Nicolls told me that you could not turn the soil anywhere in the neighbourhood without coming upon human bones, bones of men who had been murdered coming away from the diggings with gold.

As Mrs. Nicolls had a great deal of business to see to with regard to selling her house and furniture, I did not make any stay with her at Sandringham. Some years later we met in London. She was much altered; she had never got over the loss of her husband, for they had been devotedly attached to each other. She was then returning to Australia. I shall never forget the happy days when camping in the bush near Melbourne.

On leaving Sandringham I made for Wollongong to see some old friends with whom I had stayed ten years previously. While in the wilds of the bush, I alighted from my bicycle to get some tea at a small wayside accommodation house. I had already ridden seventy miles, so was much in need of some refreshment. The place was kept by a widow and her daughter. The landlady was unable to get me any tea, as there was no boiling water ready, so I asked for some wine. The wine made me disinclined to go farther, so I decided to stay for the night, as the place seemed nice and clean and quiet.

The landlady asked me if I could play the piano, as she wanted someone to play the accompaniments to songs to amuse the men who came there in the evening after their work was done (they were working in the bush). I replied that I would be quite happy to do my best. She hardly gave me time to finish my supper before I was called to the piano. The mother and daughter sang, the admiring audience being crowded in the passage. After a song or two a drink was sent in to me from one of the audience. I assured the landlady that I could not possibly take it, so she drank it off, saying it would give great offence to refuse it. This kind attention was repeated after nearly every song, the landlady and her daughter disposing of the drinks, as I refused every time.

It was getting late and I was very tired and expressed a wish to retire. One more and ever one more song was pleaded for. Suddenly the two women rushed out of the room and locked me in! Doubtless they had gone to serve drinks at the bar before closing time. They promised, when they returned, to let me retire if I would play two more accompaniments. When finished, and quiet reigned over the establishment the two women escorted me, each with an arm linked in mine, to my room, vowing everlasting love and affection. They promised to be up early to get breakfast for me.

To save time in the morning I paid my bill overnight, for an early start meant that I should get a good way on the road before the heat of the day. My sleeping apartment was only the end of the veranda boarded up, and there were dogs outside keeping up an incessant howling. There were fleas in plenty in the bed. I did not get a wink of sleep, so made a very early start. The landlady heard me go and all I saw of her was her head at the window when she called out "Goodbye." The audience of the previous evening's concert were lying rolled in their blankets under the gum trees, fast asleep.

Towards evening I came to a broad, but at the time shallow, river which I wanted to cross. A "swagger" was seated on the bank preparing his supper. I asked him to carry my bicycle across the river for me. When we reached the other side, he suggested that I should return and share his supper with him. As I liked the man, and the novelty of the situation took my fancy, I accepted his invitation with thanks. He made a comfortable seat for me on his swag. When the "billy" came to the boil he added dried vegetables to the meat that was already in the can, and when sufficiently cooked we "fell to." That stew, washed down by tea, constituted our meal. I enjoyed both the meal and the conversation.

To get to Wollongong I had left the main road, that was very good, and turned down the Macquarie Valley. As it was a Sunday and accommodation and food uncertain, I took a good meal before leaving the main road. It was late in the afternoon, and on enquiring what accommodation I should find for the night, I was told of a house where paying guests could be put up. The Macquarie Valley is a show place, the scenery being very fine. It is a favourite route for Sunday drives. I met several parties, and they all told me the same tale, i.e. that at a certain house I could be taken in as a paying guest. The road was indifferent and muddy, and water had to be crossed frequently. It was beginning to get dark when I arrived at the house I had been directed to.

Very unfriendly dogs met me at the gate, and a silent boy pointed to a lady and gentleman sitting in the garden. I went up to them and asked if they could put me up for the night. The man asked who sent me, and was furious when I said that everyone on the road had told me they took in paying guests. The man simply raved and said he must have enemies to have dared to say such a thing. When he ceased raving, I asked if he intended that I should sleep by the roadside, as the evening was coming on and I could not possibly cross the muddy water in the dark. I told him I was bound for Wollongong and expected to stay with old friends there. He asked me the name of my friends, and I said, "Dr. Lee and his family." Whereupon he exclaimed, "Dr. Lee is an old friend of mine." In fact, Dr. Lee's family and his had been lately intermarried.

The wife had kept silent during this altercation, but after we discovered that we had mutual friends she led me off to the house. They were without a servant, so the husband was loath to put his wife to any more trouble, but when they discovered that I did not want any supper, that quite smoothed matters over, and she left me with her husband while she prepared a room for me. He meanwhile regaled me on passion-flower fruit.

On going to bed, the lady and I arranged that the first who was awake was to call the other, as she wanted to get the household washing over before the heat of the day, and I for the same reason wanted to make an early start. I had to guess the time, as I had no matches to look at my watch. It was only 2 a.m. when I knocked at my hostess's door, so she undertook to do the calling, and I retired to bed again. We had breakfast together about 6 a.m., and I started off, feeling most grateful for my night's lodging, and she went to the wash-tub.

As my friends in Wollongong were not expecting me, they were much astonished to see me arrive on a bicycle. It was about ten years since we had last met, and great changes had taken place. The parents were aged, the children grown up, and some of them married. I spent a few happy days with them and then rode on to Sydney. The heat was intense, often 120° in the shade. The flies tormented me terribly. I could not ride away from them. Men cycling in front of me had so many flies on their coats that I could not detect the colour of the cloth.

Through one district that I rode there was a drought that had been of long duration. The few living cattle I saw were mere skeletons. I saw one poor beast eating manure off the road. The air reeked with the smell of dead animals. I suffered dreadfully from thirst. I begged a drink from a roadside house, and was given a pannikin and sent to the rainwater tank and very grudgingly told to get a drink. The water was warm and not at all refreshing. Fortunately I had a supply of grapes in my basket, and

I kept the skins in my mouth as long as I could so as to keep it closed.

I had been warned of this heat by a doctor nephew who practised in Gawler in South Australia. He had written begging me not to ride through that district. There was not a blade of grass or anything green anywhere. When the rain does come in those districts, everything becomes green and grows as if by magic.

By the time I arrived at Sydney the weather had become cooler. After a pleasant stay with friends there I took the boat back to Melbourne, and from there started to cycle to Gawler, to stay with my nephew and his wife and children, but could not manage to ride the whole way, as a desert had to be crossed, and my tyres were too worn to venture. I believe that all that district which was then desert is now cultivated and inhabited.

I arrived at Gawler early one Sunday morning. My nephew and his wife were not up, but I found and made friends with their two little boys. They were very shy, so our friendship advanced but slowly.

Situated near Gawler is the Agricultural College. Mr. Jameson, the lecturer on chemistry, was a near neighbour of my nephew. Mr. Jameson cycled to the College every day, and I often went with him. The site of the College was the poorest land that could be found. It had been selected by the Government in order to see what science could do to improve it. I learned that in its native state the soil only produced seventeen bushels of wheat to the acre, and that a fertiliser consisting of sulphuric acid and a native rock brought the crop of wheat up to forty bushels to the acre. Wine was also being made at the College, and there were many other interesting things to be seen. The College prize giving came off while I was at Gawler, to which we went. I was able to indulge in some bridge, as my nephew was a good player, and two more keen players lived near and joined us.

From Adelaide I took a Messageries steamer home, calling at the usual ports.

CHAPTER XVI

THE ANTIPODES ONCE MORE

IN the autumn of 1913 I made my last trip to New Zealand. I went by a "one-class" P.&0. steamer, and the food was simply vile. One passenger, who had been matron in charge of emigrants, said she had sufficient influence to get things altered; at any rate, so far that we should be fed according to the bill of fare. Her complaints led to her being given her meals apart, where she got decent food. I was quite unable to eat any of the courses brought round at dinner, so I asked for a piece of cheese and made my dinner in future off bread and cheese. I too could have had my dinner apart, but did not care to do so. By purchases at the ports we stopped at I made up for the deficiencies and arrived at Adelaide in good health.

The nephew I had stayed with in Gawler had moved to Adelaide. At Gawler he had kept a small carriage and a pair of ponies for the children, now increased to three in number. He had some small saddles, as he wished the children to learn to ride. The saddles he had taken to Adelaide with him. My nephew was now going on his rounds in a motorcar, and had a chauffeur instead of a groom. The children were longing for their ponies, and their father not having time to look out for a quiet one for them, I offered to get one and teach the children to ride. I went to the sale yards where the ponies from Kangaroo Island were put up to auction, but found I should have to bid for a whole truck load – single ones were not sold.

I saw an advertisement in a daily paper of a quiet pony used to children. I went in search of it, and found it as described. The little girl who had been riding it crawled between its legs and proved to me it was quite suitable. My little nephews were rather timid, but their small sister made the most of the pony. Soon she and the boys and a girlfriend and the two maids were taking it in turn to ride in a paddock at the back of the house. On hearing shouts of laughter one day, we found the pony drawing the clothes basket, with the terrier on his back.

Melbourne was my next stopping place, where I stayed with the Jamesons. Mr. Jameson had been promoted from the College at Gawler to a better appointment in Melbourne. The Jamesons took me to a little place in the country where they used to spend weekends, and there we led a picnic life. The weather was favourable, and I well remember "Fern Tree Gully."

From Melbourne I crossed to New Zealand. I was in my seventieth year. When I arrived there I was delighted to find that I could still walk and climb mountains with the same ease and enjoyment as my younger friends. From New Plymouth I went to Mount Egmont. A cousin's wife lent me her bicycle, and her son accompanied me. We spent the night in the huts at the foot of the mountains. We had passed through a lovely piece of bush where the rata[8] was in full blossom. We started early the following morning after consulting a guide as to which spur of the mountain we should follow. It was a beautiful, clear day and the track was quite good till we got to the glacier. Then all tracks ceased. I could only get a foothold at the edge of the moraine, and consequently made slow progress. I was taking a short rest when I let my alpenstock slip out of my hand, and it slithered down a little way, but it took me some time to regain it. Meanwhile my companion had made headway.

Soon I reached the bed of rocks that are on the top of the mountain, and I had only a very little more climbing to reach the summit and see the view on the other side, but my companion came back and said we must return immediately, as clouds were gathering. I had promised his mother most faithfully that if there was any sign of cloud or mist rising I would return directly. It was a great disappointment to me, but it would have taken me some time to climb the few yards of difficult rock to reach the summit, so we made our way down again.

---

8. A New Zealand tree with red flowers.

The descent was fairly easy. The clouds soon hid the top of the mountain from our view, but they did not overtake us.

Mount Egmont stands out quite alone in all its glory, and is visible from a great distance. The danger of climbing the mountain was because there were no definite tracks, and the mist rose so suddenly and enveloped it that it was easy to lose oneself. Many accidents had happened to climbers on the mountain, which is nearly 10,000 feet high, and very steep.

In Canterbury I did more climbing with old friends, in the neighbourhood where I spent my early married life. I was entertained by the owners of what had been our property. Great alterations had been made; a better and safer road had been constructed to the house. The owners were able to keep a motorcar; water was laid on to the house, and a bathroom built on. Part of the land was cultivated, and a splendid crop of wheat awaited the harvest. As I have before related, the owners asked me to return the following year, when they were expecting a party of scientists to visit them, to be sent by the Government to explore and report on the neighbourhood. I quite intended to accept their kind invitation, but the war broke out and put a stop to my plans.

I crossed again to Melbourne and trained on to Queensland to stay with a friend, who had recently married an Australian and lived on a cattle ranch twenty miles from Gladstone. He and his wife met me at Gladstone in their motor, and we drove to their house along a track in the bush. It was Christmas time, so not overpoweringly hot. I rode while staying with these friends, but as there were no side-saddles I had to ride astride, which was almost a new experience for me. We went out kangaroo hunting, but had no luck, although we saw a great many.

I loved being in the real wilds of Australia. It was a joy to me to see frilled lizards, snakes, and kangaroos once again, and to hear the bark of the dingoes (wild dog) at night. A litter of dingoes had been found near the house, but they had to be poisoned by one of the stockmen.

I enjoyed my stay in Queensland immensely, and from there I went to Sydney, where I made a short stay before returning to England.

CONCLUSION
ONE WOMAN'S RECORD

Shortly after my return from my last trip to New Zealand, the Great War started. I hoped to turn my knowledge of European languages to good account, but failed to obtain any appointment, probably because I did not know where or how to apply to advantage. My war work consisted in helping in canteens, and I joined needlework parties to make garments for our men at the front. I sent many parcels of small presents to our soldiers in France, including a number of puddings of my own making each Christmas.

During the War my cycling, of course, was restricted to England, but as soon as the war was over I cycled to Berlin, and shortly after my return to England, started off again for the Rhine, returning through Alsace and Lorraine.

I remained faithful to my bicycle till my eightieth year. Since then I have visited Jamaica and Tangier.

The author aged 84.

Recently I joined conducted tours to Spain and Portugal, visiting places of great interest. I still cherish the hope of revisiting New Zealand, perhaps by aeroplane. Speaking of aeroplanes, I feel sure that if "flying" had been possible in my young days, I should have taken to it, that is, if I could have afforded to do so. But perhaps it would not have given me so much enjoyment as I derived from trundling my bicycle into so many corners of the world.

If during the thirty years I was cycling I may not have established a record, for one of my age, as to mileage, I have the vanity to suppose that I have seen more of the world from the saddle of a bicycle than any other woman cyclist.

If in saying this, or elsewhere in these recollections, I appear to blow my own trumpet, please remember that I have outlived all my trumpeters, if ever I had any, and might therefore reasonably be allowed to sound a note or two myself.

Truly, my intention in writing these memoirs was to amuse, perhaps, my friends, of whom I am happy to say I have many, and who have always taken a keen interest in my excursions, and also to give such as might care to know some idea how we lived in my young days.

If I have been at times unduly prolix[9], as I fear I have, age must be my excuse. As I finish writing these words I am in my eighty-ninth year!

---

9. Long and boring